THE FUGITIVE
A PLAY IN FOUR ACTS

THE FUGITIVE

A PLAY IN FOUR ACTS

BY

JOHN GALSWORTHY

NEW YORK

CHARLES SCRIBNER'S SONS

1913

PERSONS OF THE PLAY

GEORGE DEDMOND, *a civilian*

CLARE, *his wife*

GENERAL SIR CHARLES DEDMOND, K.C.B., *his father.*

LADY DEDMOND, *his mother*

REGINALD HUNTINGDON, *Clare's brother*

EDWARD FULLARTON }
DOROTHY FULLARTON } *her friends*

PAYNTER, *a manservant*

BURNEY, *a maid*

TWISDEN, *a solicitor*

HAYWOOD, *a tobacconist*

MALISE, *a writer*

MRS. MILER, *his caretaker*

THE PORTER *at his lodgings*

A BOY *messenger*

ARNAUD, *a waiter at "The Gascony"*

MR. VARLEY, *manager of "The Gascony"*

TWO LADIES WITH LARGE HATS, A LADY AND GENTLEMAN, A
    LANGUID LORD, HIS COMPANION, A YOUNG MAN, A BLOND
    GENTLEMAN, A DARK GENTLEMAN.

ACT   I.   *George Dedmond's Flat. Evening.*

ACT II. *The rooms of Malise. Morning.*

ACT III. SCENE I. *The rooms of Malise. Late afternoon.*
           SCENE II. *The rooms of Malise. Early After-*
                 noon.

ACT IV. *A small supper room at "The Gascony."*

Between Acts I and II three nights elapse.

Between Acts II and Act III, Scene I, three months.

*Between Act III, Scene I, and Act III, Scene II, three
months.*

Between Act III, Scene II, and Act IV six months.

CAST OF THE FIRST PRODUCTION

AT THE

ROYAL COURT THEATRE, SEPTEMBER 16, 1913

George Dedmond	MR. CLAUDE KING
Clare	MISS IRENE ROOKE
General Sir Charles Dedmond, K.C.B.	MR. NIGEL PLAYFAIR
Lady Dedmond	MISS ALMA MURRAY
Reginald Huntingdon	MR. HYLTON ALLEN
Edward Fullarton	MR. LESLIE REA
Mrs. Fullarton	MISS ESTELLE WINWOOD
Paynter	MR. FRANK MACRAE
Burney	MISS DORIS BATEMAN
Twisden	MR. J. H. ROBERTS
Haywood	MR. CHARLES GROVES
Malise	MR. MILTON ROSMER
Mrs. Miler	MRS. A. B. TAPPING
Porter	MR. ERIC BARBER
A Messenger Boy	

CHARACTERS IN ACT FOUR

A Young Man	MR. VINCENT CLIVE
Arnaud	MR. CLARENCE DERWENT
Mr. Varley	MR. CHARLES GROVES
A Languid Lord	MR. J. H. ROBERTS
His Companion	MISS MORE-DUNPHIE
A Blond Gentleman	MR. LESLIE REA
Two Ladies with large hats	MISSES BATEMAN and NEWCOMBE

"With a hey-ho chivy—
Hark-forrard, hark-forrard, tantivy!"

ACT I

The SCENE *is the pretty drawing-room of a flat. There are two doors, one open into the hall, the other shut and curtained. Through a large bay window, the curtains of which are not yet drawn, the towers of Westminster can be seen darkening in a summer sunset; a grand piano stands across one corner. The man-servant* PAYNTER, *clean-shaven and discreet, is arranging two tables for Bridge.*

BURNEY, *the maid, a girl with one of those flowery Botticellian faces only met with in England, comes in through the curtained door, which she leaves open, disclosing the glimpse of a white wall.* PAYNTER *looks up at her; she shakes her head, with an expression of concern.*

PAYNTER. Where's she gone?

BURNEY. Just walks about, I fancy.

PAYNTER. She and the Governor don't hit it! One of these days she'll flit—you'll see. I like her—she's a lady; but these throughbred 'uns—it's their skin and their mouths. They'll go till they drop if they like the job, and if they don't, it's nothing but jib—jib—jib. How was it down there before she married him?

BURNEY. Oh! Quiet, of course.

1

PAYNTER. Country homes—I know 'em. What's
her father, the old Rector, like?

BURNEY. Oh! very steady old man.   The mother
dead long before I took the place.

PAYNTER. Not a penny, I suppose?

BURNEY. [*Shaking her head*] No; and seven of them.

PAYNTER. [*At sound of the hall door*] The Governor!

> BURNEY *withdraws through the curtained door.*
>
> GEORGE DEDMOND *enters from the hall.   He is
> in evening dress, opera hat, and overcoat; his
> face is broad, comely, glossily shaved, but with
> neat moustaches.   His eyes, clear, small, and
> blue-grey, have little speculation.   His hair is
> well brushed.*

GEORGE. [*Handing* PAYNTER *his coat and hat*] Look
here, Paynter!   When I send up from the Club for my
dress things, always put in a black waistcoat as well.

PAYNTER. I asked the mistress, sir.

GEORGE. In future—see?

PAYNTER. Yes, sir. [*Signing towards the window*] Shall
I leave the sunset, sir?

> But GEORGE *has crossed to the curtained door;
> he opens it and says:* "Clare!"   *Receiving no
> answer, he goes in.*   PAYNTER *switches up the
> electric light.   His face, turned towards the cur-
> tained door, is apprehensive.*

GEORGE. [*Re-entering*] Where's Mrs. Dedmond?

PAYNTER. I hardly know, sir.

GEORGE. Dined in?

PAYNTER. She had a mere nothing at seven, sir.

GEORGE. Has she gone out, since?

PAYNTER. Yes, sir—that is, yes. The—er—mistress was not dressed at all. A little matter of fresh air, I think, sir.

GEORGE. What time did my mother say they'd be here for Bridge?

PAYNTER. Sir Charles and Lady Dedmond were coming at half-past nine; and Captain Huntingdon, too—Mr. and Mrs. Fullarton might be a bit late, sir.

GEORGE. It's that now. Your mistress said nothing?

PAYNTER. Not to me, sir.

GEORGE. Send Burney.

PAYNTER. Very good, sir.   [*He withdraws.*

> GEORGE *stares gloomily at the card tables.* BURNEY *comes in from the hall.*

GEORGE. Did your mistress say anything before she went out?

BURNEY. Yes, sir.

GEORGE. Well?

BURNEY. I don't think she meant it, sir.

GEORGE. I don't want to know what you don't think, I want the fact.

BURNEY. Yes, sir. The mistress said: "I hope it'll be a pleasant evening, Burney!"

GEORGE. Oh!—Thanks.

BURNEY. I've put out the mistress's things, sir.

GEORGE. Ah!

BURNEY. Thank you, sir.   [*She withdraws.*

GEORGE. Damn!

> *He again goes to the curtained door, and passes through.* PAYNTER, *coming in from the hall, announces:* "General Sir Charles and Lady Dedmond." SIR CHARLES *is an upright, well-groomed, grey-moustached, red-faced man of sixty-seven, with a keen eye for molehills, and none at all for mountains.* LADY DEDMOND *has a firm, thin face, full of capability and decision, not without kindliness; and faintly weathered, as if she had faced many situations in many parts of the world. She is fifty-five.*
>
> PAYNTER *withdraws.*

SIR CHARLES. Hullo! Where are they? H'm!

> *As he speaks,* GEORGE *re-enters.*

LADY DEDMOND. [*Kissing her son*] Well, George. Where's Clare?

GEORGE. Afraid she's late.

LADY DEDMOND. Are we early?

GEORGE. As a matter of fact, she's not in.

LADY DEDMOND. Oh?

SIR CHARLES. H'm! Not—not had a rumpus?

GEORGE. Not particularly. [*With the first real sign of feeling*] What I can't stand is being made a fool of before other people. Ordinary friction one can put up with. But that——

SIR CHARLES. Gone out on purpose? What!

LADY DEDMOND. What was the trouble?

GEORGE. I told her this morning you were coming in

to Bridge. Appears she'd asked that fellow Malise, for music.

LADY DEDMOND. Without letting you know?

GEORGE. I believe she did tell me.

LADY DEDMOND. But surely——

GEORGE. I don't want to discuss it. There's never anything in particular. We're all anyhow, as you know.

LADY DEDMOND. I see. [*She looks shrewdly at her son*] My dear, I should be rather careful about him, I think.

SIR CHARLES. Who's that?

LADY DEDMOND. That Mr. Malise.

SIR CHARLES. Oh! That chap!

GEORGE. Clare isn't that sort.

LADY DEDMOND. I know. But she catches up notions very easily. I think it's a great pity you ever came across him.

SIR CHARLES. Where did you pick him up?

GEORGE. Italy—this Spring—some place or other where they couldn't speak English.

SIR CHARLES. Um! That's the worst of travellin'.

LADY DEDMOND. I think you ought to have dropped him. These literary people— [*Quietly*] From exchanging ideas to something else, isn't very far, George.

SIR CHARLES. We'll make him play Bridge. Do him good, if he's that sort of fellow.

LADY DEDMOND. Is anyone else coming?

GEORGE. Reggie Huntingdon, and the Fullartons.

LADY DEDMOND. [*Softly*] You know, my dear boy,

I've been meaning to speak to you for a long time. It *is* such a pity you and Clare— What is it?

GEORGE. God knows! I try, and I believe she does.

SIR CHARLES. It's distressin' for us, you know, my dear fellow—distressin'.

LADY DEDMOND. I know it's been going on for a long time.

GEORGE. Oh! leave it alone, mother.

LADY DEDMOND. But, George, I'm afraid this man has brought it to a point—put ideas into her head.

GEORGE. You can't dislike him more than I do. But there's nothing one can object to.

LADY DEDMOND. Could Reggie Huntingdon do anything, now he's home? Brothers sometimes——

GEORGE. I can't bear my affairs being messed about with.

LADY DEDMOND. Well! it would be better for you and Clare to be supposed to be out together, than for her to be out alone. Go quietly into the dining-room and wait for her.

SIR CHARLES. Good! Leave your mother to make up something. She'll do it!

[*A bell sounds.*

LADY DEDMOND. That may be he. Quick!

GEORGE *goes out into the hall, leaving the door open in his haste.* LADY DEDMOND, *following, calls* "Paynter!" PAYNTER *enters.*

LADY DEDMOND. Don't say anything about your master and mistress being out. I'll explain.

PAYNTER. The master, my lady?

LADY DEDMOND. Yes, I know. But you needn't
say so. Do you understand?

PAYNTER. [*In polite dudgeon*] Just so, my lady.

[*He goes out.*

SIR CHARLES. By Jove! That fellow smells a rat!

LADY DEDMOND. Be careful, Charles!

SIR CHARLES. I should think so.

LADY DEDMOND. I shall simply say they're dining
out, and that we're not to wait Bridge for them.

SIR CHARLES. [*Listening*] He's having a palaver
with that man of George's.

> PAYNTER, *reappearing, announces:* "Captain
> Huntingdon." SIR CHARLES *and* LADY DED-
> MOND *turn to him with relief.*

LADY DEDMOND. Ah! It's you, Reginald!

HUNTINGDON. [*A tall, fair soldier, of thirty*] How
d'you do? How are you, sir? What's the matter
with their man?

SIR CHARLES. What!

HUNTINGDON. I was going into the dining-room to
get rid of my cigar; and he said: "Not in there, sir.
The master's there, but my instructions are to the
effect that he's not."

SIR CHARLES. I knew that fellow——

LADY DEDMOND. The fact is, Reginald, Clare's out,
and George is waiting for her. It's so important
people shouldn't——

HUNTINGDON. Rather!

> *They draw together, as people do, discussing the
> misfortunes of members of their families.*

LADY DEDMOND. It's getting serious, Reginald. I don't know what's to become of them. You don't think the Rector—you don't think your father would speak to Clare?

HUNTINGDON. Afraid the Governor's hardly well enough. He takes anything of that sort to heart so —especially Clare.

SIR CHARLES. Can't you put in a word yourself?

HUNTINGDON. Don't know where the mischief lies.

SIR CHARLES. I'm sure George doesn't gallop her on the road. Very steady-goin' fellow, old George.

HUNTINGDON. Oh, yes; George is all right, sir.

LADY DEDMOND. They ought to have had children.

HUNTINGDON. Expect they're pretty glad now they haven't. I really don't know what to say, ma'am.

SIR CHARLES. Saving your presence, you know, Reginald, I've often noticed parsons' daughters grow up queer. Get too much morality and rice puddin'.

LADY DEDMOND. [*With a clear look*] Charles!

SIR CHARLES. What was she like when you were kids?

HUNTINGDON. Oh, all right. Could be rather a little devil, of course, when her monkey was up.

SIR CHARLES. I'm fond of her. Nothing she wants that she hasn't got, is there?

HUNTINGDON. Never heard her say so.

SIR CHARLES. [*Dimly*] I don't know whether old George is a bit too matter of fact for her. H'm?

[*A short silence.*

LADY DEDMOND. There's a Mr. Malise coming here to-night. I forget if you know him.

HUNTINGDON. Yes. Rather a thorough-bred mongrel.

LADY DEDMOND. He's literary. [*With hesitation*] You —you don't think he—puts—er—ideas into her head?

HUNTINGDON. I asked Greyman, the novelist, about him; seems he's a bit of an Ishmaelite, even among those fellows. Can't see Clare——

LADY DEDMOND. No. Only, the great thing is that she shouldn't be encouraged. Listen!—It *is* her— coming in. I can hear their voices. Gone to her room. What a blessing that man isn't here yet! [*The door bell rings*] Tt! There he is, I expect.

SIR CHARLES. What are we goin' to say?

HUNTINGDON. Say they're dining out, and we're not to wait Bridge for them.

SIR CHARLES. Good!

> *The door is opened, and* PAYNTER *announces* "Mr. Kenneth Malise." MALISE *enters. He is a tall man, about thirty-five, with a strongly-marked, dark, irregular, ironic face, and eyes which seem to have needles in their pupils. His thick hair is rather untidy, and his dress clothes not too new.*

LADY DEDMOND. How do you do? My son and daughter-in-law are so very sorry. They'll be here directly.

> [MALISE *bows with a queer, curly smile.*

SIR CHARLES. [*Shaking hands*] How d'you do, sir?

HUNTINGDON. We've met, I think.

> *He gives* MALISE *that peculiar smiling stare,*
> *which seems to warn the person bowed to of the*
> *sort of person he is.* MALISE'S *eyes sparkle.*

LADY DEDMOND. Clare will be so grieved. One of those invitations——

MALISE. On the spur of the moment.

SIR CHARLES. You play Bridge, sir?

MALISE. Afraid not!

SIR CHARLES. Don't mean that? Then we shall have to wait for 'em.

LADY DEDMOND. I forget, Mr. Malise—you write, don't you?

MALISE. Such is my weakness.

LADY DEDMOND. Delightful profession.

SIR CHARLES. Doesn't tie you! What!

MALISE. Only by the head.

SIR CHARLES. I'm always thinkin' of writin' my experiences.

MALISE. Indeed!

> [*There is the sound of a door banged.*

SIR CHARLES. [*Hastily*] You smoke, Mr. Malise?

MALISE. Too much.

SIR CHARLES. Ah! Must smoke when you think a lot.

MALISE. Or think when you smoke a lot.

SIR CHARLES. [*Genially*] Don't know that I find that.

LADY DEDMOND. [*With her clear look at him*] Charles!

> *The door is opened.* CLARE DEDMOND *in a*

*cream-coloured evening frock comes in from the
hall, followed by* GEORGE. *She is rather pale,
of middle height, with a beautiful figure, wavy
brown hair, full, smiling lips, and large grey
mesmeric eyes, one of those women all vibration,
iced over with a trained stoicism of voice and
manner.*

LADY DEDMOND. Well, my dear!

SIR CHARLES. Ah! George.   Good dinner?

GEORGE. [*Giving his hand to* MALISE] How are you?
Clare! Mr. Malise!

CLARE. [*Smiling—in a clear voice with the faintest
possible lisp*] Yes, we met on the door-mat.   [*Pause.*

SIR CHARLES. Deuce you did!   [*An awkward pause.*

LADY DEDMOND. [*Acidly*] Mr. Malise doesn't play
Bridge, it appears.   Afraid we shall be rather in the
way of music.

SIR CHARLES. What!   Aren't we goin' to get a game?
                        [PAYNTER *has entered with a tray.*

GEORGE. Paynter!   Take that table into the dining-
room.

PAYNTER. [*Putting down the tray on a table behind
the door*] Yes, sir.

MALISE. Let me give you a hand.

> PAYNTER *and* MALISE *carry one of the Bridge
> tables out,* GEORGE *making a half-hearted at-
> tempt to relieve* MALISE.

SIR CHARLES. Very fine sunset!

> *Quite softly* CLARE *begins to laugh. All look
> at her first with surprise, then with offence,*

then almost with horror. GEORGE *is about to go up to her, but* HUNTINGDON *heads him off.*

HUNTINGDON. Bring the tray along, old man.

GEORGE *takes up the tray, stops to look at* CLARE, *then allows* HUNTINGDON *to shepherd him out.*

LADY DEDMOND. [*Without looking at* CLARE] Well, if we're going to play, Charles?   [*She jerks his sleeve.*

SIR CHARLES. What?   [*He marches out.*

LADY DEDMOND. [*Meeting* MALISE *in the doorway*] Now you will be able to have your music.

    [*She follows the* GENERAL *out.*

    [CLARE *stands perfectly still, with her eyes closed.*

MALISE. Delicious!

CLARE. [*In her level, clipped voice*] Perfectly beastly of me! I'm so sorry. I simply can't help running amok to-night.

MALISE. Never apologize for being fey. It's much too rare.

CLARE. On the door-mat! And they'd whitewashed me so beautifully! Poor dears! I wonder if I ought——

    [*She looks towards the door.*

MALISE. Don't spoil it!

CLARE. I'd been walking up and down the Embankment for about three hours. One does get desperate sometimes.

MALISE. Thank God for that!

CLARE. Only makes it worse afterwards. It seems so frightful to them, too.

MALISE. [*Softly and suddenly, but with a difficulty*

in finding the right words] Blessed be the respectable!
May they dream of—me! And blessed be all men of
the world! May they perish of ·a surfeit of—good
form!

CLARE. I like that. Oh, won't there be a row!
[*With a faint movement of her shoulders*] And the usual
reconciliation.

MALISE. Mrs. Dedmond, there's a whole world outside yours. Why don't you spread your wings?

CLARE. My dear father's a saint, and he's getting
old and frail; and I've got a sister engaged; and three
little sisters to whom I'm supposed to set a good ex-
ample. Then, I've no money, and I can't do anything
for a living, except serve in a shop. I shouldn't be
free, either; so what's the good? Besides, I oughtn't
to have married if I wasn't going to be happy. You
see, I'm not a bit misunderstood or ill-treated. It's
only——

MALISE. Prison. Break out!

CLARE. [*Turning to the window*] Did you see the
sunset? That white cloud trying to fly up?

[*She holds up her bare arms, with a motion of flight.*

MALISE. [*Admiring her*] Ah-h-h! [*Then, as she drops
her arms suddenly*] Play me something.

CLARE. [*Going to the piano*] I'm awfully grateful to
you. *You* don't make me feel just an attractive fe-
male. I wanted somebody like that. [*Letting her hands
rest on the notes*] All the same, I'm *glad* not to be
ugly.

MALISE. Thank God for beauty!

PAYNTER. [*Opening the door*] Mr. and Mrs. Fullarton.

MALISE. Who are *they?*

CLARE. [*Rising*] She's my chief pal. He was in the Navy.

> *She goes forward.* MRS. FULLARTON *is a rather tall woman, with dark hair and a quick eye. He, one of those clean-shaven naval men of good presence who have retired from the sea, but not from their susceptibility.*

MRS. FULLARTON. [*Kissing* CLARE, *and taking in both* MALISE *and her husband's look at* CLARE] We've only come for a minute.

CLARE. They're playing Bridge in the dining-room. Mr. Malise doesn't play. Mr. Malise—Mrs. Fullarton, Mr. Fullarton.

> [*They greet.*

FULLARTON. Most awfully jolly dress, Mrs. Dedmond.

MRS. FULLARTON. Yes, lovely, Clare. [FULLARTON *abases eyes which mechanically readjust themselves*] We can't stay for Bridge, my dear; I just wanted to see you a minute, that's all. [*Seeing* HUNTINGDON *coming in she speaks in a low voice to her husband*] Edward, I want to speak to Clare. How d'you do, Captain Huntingdon?

MALISE. I'll say good-night.

> *He shakes hands with* CLARE, *bows to* MRS. FULLARTON, *and makes his way out.* HUNTINGDON *and* FULLARTON *foregather in the doorway.*

MRS. FULLARTON. How *are* things, Clare? [CLARE *just moves her shoulders*] Have you done what I suggested? Your room?

CLARE. No.

MRS. FULLARTON. Why not?

CLARE. I don't want to torture him. If I strike— I'll go clean. I expect I *shall* strike.

MRS. FULLARTON. My dear! You'll have the whole world against you.

CLARE. Even you won't back me, Dolly?

MRS. FULLARTON. Of course I'll back you, all that's possible, but I can't invent things.

CLARE. You wouldn't let me come to you for a bit, till I could find my feet?

> MRS. FULLARTON, *taken aback, cannot refrain*
> *from her glance at* FULLARTON *automatically*
> *gazing at* CLARE *while he talks with* HUNT-
> INGDON.

MRS. FULLARTON. Of course—the only thing is that——

CLARE. [*With a faint smile*] It's all right, Dolly. I'm not coming.

MRS. FULLARTON. Oh! don't do anything desperate, Clare—you are so desperate sometimes. You ought to make terms—not tracks.

CLARE. Haggle? [*She shakes her head*] What have I got to make terms with? What he still wants is just what I hate giving.

MRS. FULLARTON. But, Clare——

CLARE. No, Dolly; even you don't understand.   All
day and every day—just as far apart as we can be—
and still— Jolly, isn't it? If you've got a soul at all.

MRS. FULLARTON. It's awful, really.

CLARE. I suppose there are lots of women who feel
as I do, and go on with it; only, you see, I happen to
have something in me that—comes to an end.   Can't
endure beyond a certain time, ever.

> She has taken a flower from her dress, and sud-
> denly tears it to bits. It is the only sign of
> emotion she has given.

MRS. FULLARTON. [Watching] Look here, my child;
this won't do.   You must get a rest.   Can't Reggie
take you with him to India for a bit?

CLARE. [Shaking her head] Reggie lives on his pay.

MRS. FULLARTON. [With one of her quick looks] That
was Mr. Malise, then?

FULLARTON. [Coming towards them] I say, Mrs. Dedmond, you wouldn't sing me that little song you sang
the other night, [He hums] "If I might be the falling
bee and kiss thee all the day"? Remember?

MRS. FULLARTON. "The falling dew," Edward.   We
simply must go, Clare.   Good-night.   [She kisses her.

FULLARTON. [Taking half-cover between his wife and
CLARE] It suits you down to the ground—that dress.

CLARE. Good-night.

> HUNTINGDON sees them out. Left alone CLARE
> clenches her hands, moves swiftly across to the
> window, and stands looking out.

HUNTINGDON. [Returning] Look here, Clare!

CLARE. Well, Reggie?

HUNTINGDON. This is working up for a mess, old girl. You can't do this kind of thing with impunity. No man'll put up with it. If you've got anything against George, better tell me. [CLARE *shakes her head*] You ought to know I should stick by you. What is it? Come?

CLARE. Get married, and find out after a year that she's the wrong person; so wrong that you can't exchange a single real thought; that your blood runs cold when she kisses you—then you'll know.

HUNTINGDON. My dear old girl, I don't want to be a brute; but it's a bit difficult to believe in that, except in novels.

CLARE. Yes, incredible, when you haven't tried.

HUNTINGDON. I mean, you—you chose him yourself. No one forced you to marry him.

CLARE. It does seem monstrous, doesn't it?

HUNTINGDON. My dear child, do give us a reason.

CLARE. Look! [*She points out at the night and the darkening towers*] If George saw that for the first time he'd just say, "Ah, Westminster! Clock Tower! Can you see the time by it?" As if one cared where or what it was—beautiful like that! Apply that to every —every—everything.

HUNTINGDON. [*Staring*] George may be a bit prosaic. But, my dear old girl, if that's all——

CLARE. It's not all—it's nothing. I can't explain, Reggie—it's not reason, at all; it's—it's like being underground in a damp cell; it's like knowing you'll never get out. Nothing coming—never anything coming again—never anything.

HUNTINGDON. [*Moved and puzzled*] My dear old thing; you mustn't get into fantods like this. If it's like that, don't think about it.

CLARE. When every day and every night!— Oh! I know it's my fault for having married him, but that doesn't help.

HUNTINGDON. Look here! It's not as if George wasn't quite a decent chap. And it's no use blinking things; you *are* absolutely dependent on him. At home they've got every bit as much as they can do to keep going.

CLARE. I know.

HUNTINGDON. And you've got to think of the girls. Any trouble would be very beastly for them. And the poor old Governor would feel it awfully.

CLARE. If I didn't know all that, Reggie, I should have gone home long ago.

HUNTINGDON. Well, what's to be done? If my pay would run to it—but it simply won't.

CLARE. Thanks, old boy, of course not.

HUNTINGDON. Can't you try to see George's side of it a bit?

CLARE. I *do*. Oh! don't let's talk about it.

HUNTINGDON. Well, my child, there's just one thing —you won't go sailing near the wind, will you? I mean, there are fellows always on the lookout.

CLARE. "That chap, Malise, you'd better avoid him!" Why?

HUNTINGDON. Well! I don't know him. He may be all right, but he's not our sort. And you're too pretty to go on the tack of the New Woman and that kind of thing—haven't been brought up to it.

CLARE. British home-made summer goods, light and attractive—don't wear long. [*At the sound of voices in the hall*] They seem to be going, Reggie.

[HUNTINGDON *looks at her, vexed, unhappy*.

HUNTINGDON. Don't head for trouble, old girl. Take a pull. Bless you! Good-night.

CLARE *kisses him, and when he has gone turns away from the door, holding herself in, refusing to give rein to some outburst of emotion. Suddenly she sits down at the untouched Bridge table, leaning her bare elbows on it and her chin on her hands, quite calm.* GEORGE *is coming in.* PAYNTER *follows him.*

CLARE. Nothing more wanted, thank you, Paynter. You can go home, and the maids can go to bed.

PAYNTER. We are much obliged, ma'am.

CLARE. I ran over a dog, and had to get it seen to.

PAYNTER. Naturally, ma'am!

CLARE. Good-night.

PAYNTER. I couldn't get you a little anything, ma'am?

CLARE. No, thank you.

PAYNTER. No, ma'am. Good-night, ma'am.

[*He withdraws.*

GEORGE. You needn't have gone out of your way to tell a lie that wouldn't deceive a guinea-pig. [*Going up to her*] Pleased with yourself to-night? [CLARE *shakes her head*] Before that fellow Malise; as if our own people weren't enough!

CLARE. Is it worth while to rag me? I know I've behaved badly, but I couldn't help it, really!

GEORGE. Couldn't help behaving like a shop-girl? My God! You were brought up as well as I was.

CLARE. Alas!

GEORGE. To let everybody see that we don't get on —there's only one word for it—Disgusting!

CLARE. I know.

GEORGE. Then why do you do it? I've always kept *my* end up. Why in heaven's name do you behave in this crazy way?

CLARE. I'm sorry.

GEORGE. [*With intense feeling*] You like making a fool of me!

CLARE. No— Really! Only—I must break out sometimes.

GEORGE. There are things one does not do.

CLARE. I came in because I was sorry.

GEORGE. And at once began to do it again! It seems to me you delight in rows.

CLARE. You'd miss your—reconciliations.

GEORGE. For God's sake, Clare, drop cynicism!

CLARE. And truth?

GEORGE. You are my wife, I suppose.

CLARE. And they twain shall be one—spirit.

GEORGE. Don't talk wild nonsense!

[*There is silence.*

CLARE. [*Softly*] I *don't* give satisfaction.   Please give me notice!

GEORGE. Pish!

CLARE. Five years, and four of them like this! I'm sure we've served our time. Don't you really think we might get on better together—if I went away?

GEORGE. I've told you I won't stand a separation for no real reason, and have your name bandied about all over London. I have some primitive sense of honour.

CLARE. You mean *your* name, don't you?

GEORGE. Look here.   Did that fellow Malise put all this into your head?

CLARE. No; my own evil nature.

GEORGE. I wish the deuce we'd never met him. Comes of picking up people you know nothing of. I distrust him—and his looks—and his infernal satiric way. He can't even dress decently. He's not—good form.

CLARE. [*With a touch of rapture*] Ah-h!

GEORGE. Why do you let him come? What d'you find interesting in him?

CLARE. A mind.

GEORGE. Deuced funny one! To have a mind—as you call it—it's not necessary to talk about Art and Literature.

CLARE. We don't.

GEORGE. Then what do you talk about—your minds? [CLARE *looks at him*] Will you answer a straight question? Is he falling in love with you?

CLARE. You had better ask him.

GEORGE. I tell you plainly, as a man of the world, I don't believe in the guide, philosopher and friend business.

CLARE. Thank you.

> *A silence.* CLARE *suddenly clasps her hands behind her head.*

CLARE. Let me go! You'd be much happier with any other woman.

GEORGE. Clare!

CLARE. I believe—I'm sure I could earn my living. Quite serious.

GEORGE. Are you mad?

CLARE. It has been done.

GEORGE. It will never be done by you—understand that!

CLARE. It really is time we parted. I'd go clean out of your life. I don't want your support unless I'm giving you something for your money.

GEORGE. Once for all, I don't mean to allow you to make fools of us both.

CLARE. But if we are already! Look at us. We go on, and on. We're a spectacle!

GEORGE. That's not my opinion; nor the opinion of anyone, so long as you behave yourself.

CLARE. That is—behave as you think right.

GEORGE. Clare, you're pretty riling.

CLARE. I don't want to be horrid. But I am in earnest this time.

GEORGE. So am I.

> [CLARE *turns to the curtained door*.

GEORGE. Look here! I'm sorry. God knows I don't want to be a brute. I know you're not happy.

CLARE. And you—are you happy?

GEORGE. I don't say I am. But why can't we be?

CLARE. I see no reason, except that you are you, and I am I.

GEORGE. We can try.

CLARE. I *have*—haven't you?

GEORGE. We used——

CLARE. I wonder!

GEORGE. You know we did.

CLARE. Too long ago—if ever.

GEORGE [*Coming closer*] I—still——

CLARE. [*Making a barrier of her hand*] You know that's only cupboard love.

GEORGE. We've got to face the facts.

CLARE. I thought I was.

GEORGE. The facts are that we're married—for better or worse, and certain things are expected of us. It's suicide for you, and folly for me, in my position, to ignore that. You have all you can reasonably want; and I don't—don't wish for any change. If you could bring anything against me—if I drank, or knocked about town, or expected too much of you. I'm not unreasonable in any way, that I can see.

CLARE. Well, I think we've talked enough.

> [*She again moves towards the curtained door*.

GEORGE. Look here, Clare; you don't mean you're

expecting me to put up with the position of a man who's neither married nor unmarried? That's simple purgatory. You ought to know.

CLARE. Yes. I haven't yet, have I?

GEORGE. Don't go like that! Do you suppose we're the only couple who've found things aren't what they thought, and have to put up with each other and make the best of it.

CLARE. Not by thousands.

GEORGE. Well, why do you imagine they do it?

CLARE. I don't know.

GEORGE. From a common sense of decency.

CLARE. Very!

GEORGE. By Jove! You can be the most maddening thing in all the world! [*Taking up a pack of cards, he lets them fall with a long slithering flutter*] After behaving as you have this evening, you might try to make some amends, I should think.

> CLARE *moves her head from side to side, as if in sight of something she could not avoid. He puts his hand on her arm.*

CLARE. No, no—no!

GEORGE. [*Dropping his hand*] Can't you make it up?

CLARE. I don't feel very Christian.

> *She opens the door, passes through, and closes it behind her.* GEORGE *steps quickly towards it, stops, and turns back into the room. He goes to the window and stands looking out; shuts it with a bang, and again contemplates the door. Moving forward, he rests his hand on the de-*

serted card table, clutching its edge, and muttering. Then he crosses to the door into the hall and switches off the light. He opens the door to go out, then stands again irresolute in the darkness and heaves a heavy sigh. Suddenly he mutters: "No!" Crosses resolutely back to the curtained door, and opens it. In the gleam of light CLARE is standing, unhooking a necklet. He goes in, shutting the door behind him with a thud.

CURTAIN.

ACT II

THE SCENE *is a large, whitewashed, disordered room,*
whose outer door opens on to a corridor and stairway.
Doors on either side lead to other rooms. On the
walls are unframed reproductions of fine pictures,
secured with tintacks. An old wine-coloured arm-
chair of low and comfortable appearance, near the
centre of the room, is surrounded by a litter of manu-
scripts, books, ink, pens and newspapers, as though
some one had already been up to his neck in labour,
though by a grandfather's clock it is only eleven.
On a smallish table close by, are sheets of paper,
cigarette ends, and two claret bottles. There are
many books on shelves, and on the floor, an over-
flowing pile, whereon rests a soft hat, and a black
knobby stick. MALISE *sits in his armchair, garbed*
in trousers, dressing-gown, and slippers, unshaved
and uncollared, writing. He pauses, smiles, lights
a cigarette, and tries the rhythm of the last sentence,
holding up a sheet of quarto MS.

MALISE. "Not a word, not a whisper of Liberty from
all those excellent frock-coated gentlemen—not a sign,
not a grimace. Only the monumental silence of their
profound deference before triumphant Tyranny."

> *While he speaks, a substantial woman, a little*
> *over middle-age, in old dark clothes and a black*

27

straw hat, enters from the corridor. She goes to a cupboard, brings out from it an apron and a Bissell broom. Her movements are slow and imperturbable, as if she had much time before her. Her face is broad and dark, with Chinese eyebrows.

MALISE. Wait, Mrs. Miler!

MRS. MILER. I'm gettin' be'ind'and, sir.

She comes and stands before him. MALISE *writes.*

MRS. MILER. There's a man 'angin' about below.

MALISE looks up ; seeing that she has roused his attention, she stops. But as soon as he is about to write again, goes on.

MRS. MILER. I see him first yesterday afternoon. I'd just been out to get meself a pennyworth o' soda, an' as I come in I passed 'im on the second floor, lookin' at me with an air of suspicion. I thought to meself at the time, I thought: You're a 'andy sort of 'ang-dog man.

MALISE. Well?

MRS. MILER. Well—peekin' down through the balusters, I see 'im lookin' at a photograft. That's a funny place, I thinks, to look at pictures—it's so dark there, ye 'ave to use yer eyesight. So I giv' a scrape with me 'eel [*She illustrates*] an' he pops it in his pocket, and puts up 'is 'and to knock at number three. I goes down an' I says: "You know there's no one lives there, don't yer?" "Ah!" 'e says with an air of innercence, "I wants the name of Smithers." "Oh!" I says, "try round the corner, number ten." "Ah!" 'e says, tactful, "much obliged." "Yes," I says, "you'll find 'im in at this time o' day. Good evenin'!" And I thinks to meself [*She closes one eye*] Rats! There's a good many corners hereabouts.

MALISE. [*With detached appreciation*] Very good, Mrs. Miler.

MRS. MILER. So this mornin', there e' was again on the first floor with 'is 'and raised, pretendin' to knock at number two. "Oh! you're still lookin' for 'im?" I says, lettin' him see I was 'is grandmother. "Ah!" 'e says, affable, "you misdirected me; it's here I've got my business." "That's lucky," I says, "cos nobody lives there neither. Good mornin'!" And I come straight up. If you want to see 'im at work you've only to go downstairs, 'e'll be on the ground floor by now, pretendin' to knock at number one. Wonderful resource!

MALISE. What's he like, this gentleman?

MRS. MILER. Just like the men you see on the front page o' the daily papers. Nasty, smooth-lookin' feller, with one o' them billycock hats you can't abide.

MALISE. Isn't he a dun?

MRS. MILER. *They* don't be'ave like that; *you* ought to know, sir. He's after no good. [*Then, after a little pause*] Ain't he to be put a stop to? If I took me time I could get 'im, innercent-like, with a jug o' water.

               [MALISE, *smiling, shakes his head.*

MALISE. You can get on now; I'm going to shave.

    He looks at the clock, and passes out into the inner
      room. MRS. MILER *gazes round her, pins up*

*her skirt, sits down in the armchair, takes off
her hat and puts it on the table, and slowly rolls
up her sleeves; then with her hands on her knees
she rests.   There is a soft knock on the door.
She gets up leisurely and moves flat-footed towards it. The door being opened* CLARE *is
revealed.*

CLARE. Is Mr. Malise in?

MRS. MILER. Yes.   But 'e's dressin'.

CLARE. Oh.

MRS. MILER. Won't take 'im long.   What name?

CLARE. Would you say—a lady.

MRS. MILER. It's against the rules.   But if you'll
sit down a moment I'll see what I can do.   [*She brings
forward a chair and rubs it with her apron.   Then goes
to the door of the inner room and speaks through it*] A
lady to see you. [*Returning she removes some cigarette
ends*] This is my hour.   I shan't make much dust.
[*Noting* CLARE's *eyebrows raised at the débris round the
armchair*] I'm particular about not disturbin' things.

CLARE. I'm sure you are.

MRS. MILER. He likes 'is 'abits regular.

*Making a perfunctory pass with the Bissell broom,
she runs it to the cupboard, comes back to the
table, takes up a bottle and holds it to the light;
finding it empty, she turns it upside down and
drops it into the wastepaper basket; then, holding up the other bottle, and finding it not empty,
she corks it and drops it into the fold of her
skirt.*

MRS. MILER. He takes his claret fresh-opened—not like these 'ere bawgwars.

CLARE. [*Rising*] I think I'll come back later.

MRS. MILER. Mr. Malise is not in my confidence. We keep each other to ourselves. Perhaps you'd like to read the paper; he has it fresh every mornin'—the *Westminister*.

> *She plucks that journal from out of the armchair and hands it to* CLARE, *who sits down again unhappily to brood.* MRS. MILER *makes a pass or two with a very dirty duster, then stands still. No longer hearing sounds,* CLARE *looks up.*

MRS. MILER. I wouldn't interrupt yer with my workin,' but 'e likes things clean. [*At a sound from the inner room*] That's 'im; 'e's cut 'isself! I'll just take 'im the tobaccer!

> *She lifts a green paper screw of tobacco from the débris round the armchair and taps on the door. It opens.* CLARE *moves restlessly across the room.*

MRS. MILER. [*Speaking into the room*] The tobaccer. The lady's waitin'.

> CLARE *has stopped before a reproduction of Titian's picture "Sacred and Profane Love."* MRS. MILER *stands regarding her with a Chinese smile.* MALISE *enters, a thread of tobacco still hanging to his cheek.*

MALISE. [*Taking* MRS. MILER'S *hat off the table and handing it to her*] Do the other room.

> [*Enigmatically she goes.*

MALISE. Jolly of you to come. Can I do anything?

CLARE. I want advice—badly.

MALISE. What! Spreading your wings?

CLARE. Yes.

MALISE. Ah! Proud to have given you *that* advice. When?

CLARE. The morning after you gave it me . . .

MALISE. Well?

CLARE. I went down to my people. I knew it would hurt my Dad frightfully, but somehow I thought I could make him see. No good. He was awfully sweet, only—he couldn't.

MALISE. [*Softly*] We English love liberty in those who don't belong to us. Yes.

CLARE. It was horrible. There were the children— and my old nurse. I could never live at home now. They'd think I was——. Impossible—utterly! I'd made up my mind to go back to my owner— And then —he came down himself. I couldn't stand it. To be hauled back and begin all over again; I simply couldn't. I watched for a chance; and ran to the station, and came up to an hotel.

MALISE. Bravo!

CLARE. I don't know—no pluck this morning! You see, I've got to earn my living—no money; only a few things I can sell. All yesterday I was walking about, looking at the women. How does anyone ever get a chance?

MALISE. Sooner than you should hurt his dignity by working, your husband would pension you off.

CLARE. If I don't go back to him I couldn't take it.

MALISE. Good!

CLARE. I've thought of nursing, but it's a long train-ing, and I do so hate watching pain. The fact is, I'm pretty hopeless; can't even do art work. I came to ask you about the stage.

MALISE. Have you ever acted? [CLARE *shakes her head*] You mightn't think so, but I've heard there's a prejudice in favour of training. There's Chorus—I don't recommend it. How about your brother?

CLARE. My brother's got nothing to spare, and he wants to get married; and he's going back to India in September. The only friend I should care to bother is Mrs. Fullarton, and she's—got a husband.

MALISE. I remember the gentleman.

CLARE. Besides, I should be besieged day and night to go back. I must lie doggo somehow.

MALISE. It makes my blood boil to think of women like you. God help all ladies without money.

CLARE. I expect I shall have to go back.

MALISE. No, no! We shall find something. Keep your soul alive at all costs. What! let him hang on to you till you're nothing but—emptiness and ache, till you lose even the power to ache. Sit in his drawing-room, pay calls, play Bridge, go out with him to din-ners, return to—duty; and feel less and less, and be less and less, and so grow old and—die!

[*The bell rings.*

MALISE. [*Looking at the door in doubt*] By the way—he'd no means of tracing you?

[*She shakes her head.*
[*The bell rings again.*

MALISE. Was there a man on the stairs as you came up?

CLARE. Yes. Why?

MALISE. He's begun to haunt them, I'm told.

CLARE. Oh! But that would mean they thought I —oh! no!

MALISE. Confidence in *me* is not excessive.

CLARE. Spying!

MALISE. Will you go in there for a minute? Or shall we let them ring—or—what? It may not be anything, of course.

CLARE. I'm not going to hide.

[*The bell rings a third time.*

MALISE. [*Opening the door of the inner room*] Mrs. Miler, just see who it is; and then go, for the present.

> MRS. MILER *comes out with her hat on, passes enigmatically to the door, and opens it. A man's voice says:* "Mr. Malise? Would you give him these cards?"

MRS. MILER. [*Re-entering*] The cards.

MALISE. Mr. Robert Twisden. Sir Charles and Lady Dedmond. [*He looks at* CLARE.

CLARE. [*Her face scornful and unmoved*] Let them come.

MALISE. [*To* MRS. MILER] Show them in!

> TWISDEN *enters—a clean-shaved, shrewd-looking man, with a fighting underlip, followed by* SIR CHARLES *and* LADY DEDMOND. MRS. MILER *goes. There are no greetings.*

TWISDEN. Mr. Malise? How do you do, Mrs. Dedmond? Had the pleasure of meeting you at your wedding. [CLARE *inclines her head*] I am Mr. George Dedmond's solicitor, sir. I wonder if you would be so very kind as to let us have a few words with Mrs. Dedmond alone?

> *At a nod from* CLARE, MALISE *passes into the inner room, and shuts the door. A silence.*

SIR CHARLES. [*Suddenly*] What!

LADY DEDMOND. Mr. Twisden, will you——?

TWISDEN. [*Uneasy*] Mrs. Dedmond——I must apologize, but you—you hardly gave us an alternative, did you? [*He pauses for an answer, and, not getting one, goes on*] Your disappearance has given your husband great anxiety. Really, my dear madam, you must forgive us for this—attempt to get into communication.

CLARE. Why did you spy ここ here?

SIR CHARLES. No, no! Nobody's spied on you. What!

TWISDEN. I'm afraid the answer is that we appear to have been justified. [*At the expression on* CLARE'S *face he goes on hastily*] Now, Mrs. Dedmond, I'm a lawyer and I know that appearances are misleading. Don't think I'm unfriendly; I wish you well. [CLARE *raises her eyes. Moved by that look, which is exactly as if she had said: "I have no friends," he hurries on*] What we want to say to you is this: Don't let this split go on! Don't commit yourself to what you'll bitterly regret. Just tell us what's the matter. I'm sure it can be put straight.

CLARE. I have nothing against my husband—it was quite unreasonable to leave him.

TWISDEN. Come, that's good.

CLARE. Unfortunately, there's something stronger than reason.

TWISDEN. I don't know it, Mrs. Dedmond.

CLARE. No?

TWISDEN. [*Disconcerted*] Are you—you oughtn't to take a step without advice, in your position.

CLARE. Nor with it?

TWISDEN. [*Approaching her*] Come, now; isn't there anything you feel you'd like to say—that might help to put matters straight?

CLARE. I don't think so, thank you.

LADY DEDMOND. You must see, Clare, that——

TWISDEN. In your position, Mrs. Dedmond—a beautiful young woman without money. I'm quite blunt. This is a hard world. Should be awfully sorry if anything goes wrong.

CLARE. And if I go back?

TWISDEN. Of two evils, if it be so—choose the least!

CLARE. I am twenty-six; he is thirty-two. We can't reasonably expect to die for fifty years.

LADY DEDMOND. That's morbid, Clare.

TWISDEN. What's open to you if you don't go back? Come, what's your position? Neither fish, flesh, nor fowl; fair game for everybody. Believe me, Mrs. Dedmond, for a pretty woman to strike, as it appears you're doing, simply because the spirit of her marriage has taken flight, is madness. You must know that no

one pays attention to anything but facts. If now—
excuse me—you—you had a lover, [*His eyes travel
round the room and again rest on her*] you would, at all
events, have some ground under your feet, some sort
of protection, but [*He pauses*] as you have not—you've
none.

CLARE. Except what I make myself.

SIR CHARLES. Good God!

TWISDEN. Yes! Mrs. Dedmond! There's the bed-
rock difficulty. As you haven't money, you should
never have been pretty.   You're up against the world,
and you'll get no mercy from it. We lawyers see too
much of that.   I'm putting it brutally, as a man of the
world.

CLARE. Thank you. Do you think you quite grasp
the alternative?

TWISDEN. [*Taken aback*] But, my dear young lady,
there are two sides to every contract. After all, your
husband's fulfilled his.

CLARE. So have I up till now. I shan't ask anything from him—nothing—do you understand?

LADY DEDMOND. But, my dear, you must live.

TWISDEN. Have you ever done any sort of work?

CLARE. Not yet.

TWISDEN. Any conception of the competition now-
adays?

CLARE. I can try.

[TWISDEN, *looking at her, shrugs his shoulders.*

CLARE. [*Her composure a little broken by that look*]
It's real to me—this—you see!

SIR CHARLES. But, my dear girl, what the devil's to become of George?

CLARE. He can do what he likes—it's nothing to me.

TWISDEN. Mrs. Dedmond, I say without hesitation you've no notion of what you're faced with, brought up to a sheltered life as you've been. Do realize that you stand at the parting of the ways, and one leads into the wilderness.

CLARE. Which?

TWISDEN. [*Glancing at the door through which* MALISE *has gone*] Of course, if you want to play at wild asses there are plenty who will help you.

SIR CHARLES. By Gad! Yes!

CLARE. I only want to breathe.

TWISDEN. Mrs. Dedmond, go back! You can now. It will be too late soon. There are lots of wolves about.

> [*Again he looks at the door.*

CLARE. But not where you think. You say I need advice. I came here for it.

TWISDEN. [*With a curiously expressive shrug*] In that case I don't know that I can usefully stay.

> [*He goes to the outer door.*

CLARE. Please don't have me followed when I leave here. Please!

LADY DEDMOND. George is outside, Clare.

CLARE. I don't wish to see him. By what right have you come here? [*She goes to the door through which* MALISE *has passed, opens it, and says*] Please come in, Mr. Malise.

> MALISE *enters.*

TWISDEN. I am sorry. [*Glancing at* MALISE, *he inclines his head*] I am sorry. Good morning. [*He goes.*

LADY DEDMOND. Mr. Malise, I'm sure, will see——

CLARE. Mr. Malise will stay here, please, in his own room. [MALISE *bows.*

SIR CHARLES. My dear girl, 'pon my soul, you know, I can't grasp your line of thought at all!

CLARE. No?

LADY DEDMOND. George is most willing to take up things just as they were before you left.

CLARE. Ah!

LADY DEDMOND. Quite frankly—what is it you want?

CLARE. To be left alone. Quite frankly, he made a mistake to have me spied on.

LADY DEDMOND. But, my good girl, if you'd let us know where you were, like a reasonable being. You can't possibly be left to yourself without money or position of any kind. Heaven knows what you'd be driven to! [*She looks at* MALISE.

MALISE. [*Softly*] Delicious!

SIR CHARLES. You will be good enough to repeat that out loud, sir.

LADY DEDMOND. Charles! Clare, you must know this is all a fit of spleen; your duty and your interest —marriage is sacred, Clare.

CLARE. Marriage! *My* marriage has become the— the reconciliation—of two animals—one of them unwilling. That's all the sanctity there is about it.

SIR CHARLES. What!

LADY DEDMOND. You ought to be horribly ashamed.

CLARE. Of the fact—I am.

LADY DEDMOND. [*Darting a glance at* MALISE] If we are to talk this out, it must be in private.

MALISE. [*To* CLARE] Do you wish me to go?

CLARE. No.

LADY DEDMOND. [*At* MALISE] I should have thought ordinary decent feeling—— Good heavens, girl! Can't you see that you're being played with?

CLARE. If you insinuate anything against Mr. Malise, you lie.

LADY DEDMOND. If you *will* do these things—come to a man's rooms——

CLARE. I came to Mr. Malise because he's the only person I know with imagination enough to see what my position is; I came to him a quarter of an hour ago, for the first time, for definite advice, and you instantly suspect him. That is disgusting.

LADY DEDMOND. [*Frigidly*] Is this the natural place for me to find my son's wife?

CLARE. His woman.

LADY DEDMOND. Will you listen to Reginald?

CLARE. I have.

LADY DEDMOND. Haven't you any religious sense at all, Clare?

CLARE. None, if it's religion to live as we do.

LADY DEDMOND. It's terrible—this state of mind! It's really terrible!

> CLARE *breaks into the soft laugh of the other evening. As if galvanized by the sound,* SIR

CHARLES *comes to life out of the transfixed bewilderment with which he has been listening.*

SIR CHARLES. For God's sake don't laugh like that!

[CLARE *stops.*

LADY DEDMOND. [*With real feeling*] For the sake of the simple right, Clare!

CLARE. Right? Whatever else is right—*our* life is not. [*She puts her hand on her heart*] I swear before God that I've tried and tried. I swear before God, that if I believed we could ever again love each other only a little tiny bit, I'd go back. I swear before God that I don't want to hurt anybody.

LADY DEDMOND. But you are hurting everybody. Do—do be reasonable!

CLARE. [*Losing control*] Can't you see that I'm fighting for all my life to come—not to be buried alive —not to be slowly smothered. Look at me! I'm not wax—I'm flesh and blood. And you want to prison me for ever—body and soul.

[*They stare at her.*

SIR CHARLES. [*Suddenly*] By Jove! I don't know, I don't know! What!

LADY DEDMOND. [*To* MALISE] If you have any decency left, sir, you will allow my son, at all events, to speak to his wife alone. [*Beckoning to her husband*] We'll wait below.

SIR CHARLES. I—I want to speak. [*To* CLARE] My dear, if you feel like this, I can only say as a—as a gentleman——

LADY DEDMOND. Charles!

SIR CHARLES. Let me alone! I can only say that
—damme, I don't know that I can say anything!

> *He looks at her very grieved, then turns and
> marches out, followed by* LADY DEDMOND,
> *whose voice is heard without, answered by his:*
> "What!" *In the doorway, as they pass,*
> GEORGE *is standing; he comes in.*

GEORGE. [*Going up to* CLARE, *who has recovered all
her self-control*] Will you come outside and speak to me?

CLARE. No.

> GEORGE *glances at* MALISE, *who is leaning
> against the wall with folded arms.*

GEORGE. [*In a low voice*] Clare!

CLARE. Well!

GEORGE. You try me pretty high, don't you, forcing
me to come here, and speak before this fellow? Most
men would think the worst, finding you like this.

CLARE. You need not have come—or thought at all.

GEORGE. Did you imagine I was going to let you
vanish without an effort——

CLARE. To save me?

GEORGE. For God's sake be just! I've come here
to say certain things. If you force me to say them
before him—on your head be it! Will you appoint
somewhere else?

CLARE. No.

GEORGE. Why not?

CLARE. I know all those "certain things." "You
must come back. It is your duty. You have no
money. Your friends won't help you. You can't earn

your living. You are making a scandal." You might even say for the moment: "Your room shall be respected."

GEORGE. Well, it's true and you've no answer.

CLARE. Oh! [*Suddenly*] Our life's a lie. It's stupid; it's disgusting. I'm tired of it! Please leave me alone!

GEORGE. You rather miss the point, I'm afraid. I didn't come here to tell you what you know perfectly well when you're sane. I came here to say this: Anyone in her senses could see the game your friend here is playing. It wouldn't take a baby in. If you think that a gentleman like that [*His stare travels round the dishevelled room till it rests on* MALISE] champions a pretty woman for nothing, you make a fairly bad mistake.

CLARE. Take care.

    But MALISE, *after one convulsive movement of his hands, has again become rigid.*

GEORGE. I don't pretend to be subtle or that kind of thing; but I have ordinary common sense. I don't attempt to be superior to plain facts——

CLARE. [*Under her breath*] Facts!

GEORGE. Oh! for goodness' sake drop that hifalutin' tone. It doesn't suit you. Look here! If you like to go abroad with one of your young sisters until the autumn, I'll let the flat and go to the Club.

CLARE. Put the fire out with a penny hose. [*Slowly*] I am not coming back to you, George. The farce is over.

GEORGE. [*Taken aback for a moment by the finality of her tone, suddenly fronts* MALISE] Then there *is* something between you and this fellow.

MALISE. [*Dangerously, but without moving*] I beg your pardon!

CLARE. There—is—nothing.

GEORGE [*Looking from one to the other*] At all events, I won't—I won't see a woman who once— [CLARE *makes a sudden effacing movement with her hands*] I won't see her go to certain ruin without lifting a finger.

CLARE. That is noble.

GEORGE. [*With intensity*] I don't know that you deserve anything of me. But on my honour, as a gentleman, I came here this morning for your sake, to warn you of what you're doing. [*He turns suddenly on* MALISE] And I tell this precious friend of yours plainly what I think of him, and that I'm not going to play into his hands.

> MALISE, *without stirring from the wall, looks at* CLARE, *and his lips move.*

CLARE. [*Shakes her head at him—then to* GEORGE] Will you go, please?

GEORGE. I will go when you do.

MALISE. A man of the world should know better than that.

GEORGE. Are you coming?

MALISE. That is inconceivable.

GEORGE. I'm not speaking to you, sir.

MALISE. You are right. Your words and mine will never kiss each other.

GEORGE. Will you come? [CLARE *shakes her head.*

GEORGE. [*With fury*] D'you mean to stay in this pigsty with that rhapsodical swine?

MALISE. [*Transformed*] By God, if you don't go, I'll kill you.

GEORGE. [*As suddenly calm*] That remains to be seen.

MALISE. [*With most deadly quietness*] Yes, I will *kill* you.

> *He goes stealthily along the wall, takes up from where it lies on the pile of books the great black knobby stick, and stealthily approaches* GEORGE, *his face quite fiendish.*

CLARE. [*With a swift movement, grasping the stick*] Please.

> MALISE *resigns the stick, and the two men, perfectly still, glare at each other.* CLARE, *letting the stick fall, puts her foot on it. Then slowly she takes off her hat and lays it on the table.*

CLARE. *Now* will you go!   [*There is silence.*

GEORGE. [*Staring at her hat*] You mad little fool! Understand this; if you've not returned home by three o'clock I'll divorce you, and you may roll in the gutter with this high-souled friend of yours. And mind this, you sir—I won't spare you—by God! Your pocket shall suffer. That's the only thing that touches fellows like you.

> *Turning, he goes out, and slams the door.* CLARE *and* MALISE *remain face to face. Her lips have begun to quiver.*

CLARE. Horrible!

> *She turns away, shuddering, and sits down on the edge of the armchair, covering her eyes with the backs of her hands. MALISE picks up the stick, and fingers it lovingly. Then putting it down, he moves so that he can see her face. She is sitting quite still, staring straight before her.*

MALISE. Nothing could be better.

CLARE. I don't know what to do! I don't know what to do!

MALISE. Thank the stars for your good fortune.

CLARE. He means to have revenge on you! And it's all my fault.

MALISE. Let him. Let him go for his divorce. Get rid of him. Have done with him—somehow.

> *She gets up and stands with face averted. Then swiftly turning to him.*

CLARE. If I must bring you harm—let me pay you back! I can't bear it otherwise! Make some use of me, if you don't mind!

MALISE. My God!

> [*She puts up her face to be kissed, shutting her eyes.*

MALISE. You poor——

> *He clasps and kisses her, then, drawing back, looks in her face. She has not moved, her eyes are still closed; but she is shivering; her lips are tightly pressed together; her hands twitching.*

MALISE. [*Very quietly*] No, no! This is not the house of a "gentleman."

CLARE. [*Letting her head fall, and almost in a whisper*]
I'm sorry.

MALISE. I understand.

CLARE. I don't feel. And without—I can't, can't.

MALISE. [*Bitterly*] Quite right. You've had enough
of *that*.

> *There is a long silence. Without looking at him*
> *she takes up her hat, and puts it on.*

MALISE. Not going?   [CLARE *nods.*

MALISE. You don't trust me?

CLARE. I *do!* But I can't take when I'm not giving.

MALISE. I beg—I beg you! What does it matter?
Use me! Get free somehow.

CLARE. Mr. Malise, I know what I ought to be to
you, if I let you in for all this. I know what you
want—or will want. Of course—why not?

MALISE. I give you my solemn word——

CLARE. No! if I can't be *that* to you—it's not real.
And I *can't*. It isn't to be manufactured, is it?

MALISE. It is not.

CLARE. To make use of you in such a way! No.

> [*She moves towards the door.*

MALISE. *Where* are you going?

> CLARE *does not answer. She is breathing rapidly.*
> *There is a change in her, a sort of excitement be-*
> *neath her calmness.*

MALISE. Not back to *him?* [CLARE *shakes her head*]
Thank God! But where? To your people again?

CLARE. No.

MALISE. Nothing—desperate?

CLARE. Oh! no.

MALISE. Then what—tell me—come!

CLARE. I don't know.   Women manage somehow.

MALISE. But *you*—poor dainty thing!

CLARE. It's all right!   Don't be unhappy!   Please!

MALISE. [*Seizing her arm*] D'you imagine they'll let you off, out there—you with your face?   Come, trust me—trust me!   You must!

CLARE. [*Holding out her hand*] Good-bye!

MALISE. [*Not taking that hand*] This great damned world, and—you!   Listen!   [*The sound of the traffic far down below is audible in the stillness*] Into that! alone—helpless—without money.   The men who work with you; the men you make friends of—d'you think they'll let you be?   The men in the streets, staring at you, stopping you—pudgy, bull-necked brutes; devils with hard eyes; senile swine; and the "chivalrous" men, like me, who don't mean you harm, but can't help seeing you're made for love!   Or suppose you *don't* take covert but struggle on in the open.   Society!   The respectable!   The pious!   Even those who love you! Will they let you be?   Hue and cry!   The hunt was joined the moment you broke away!   It will never let up!   Covert to covert—till they've run you down, and you're back in the cart, and God pity you!

CLARE. Well, I'll die running!

MALISE. No, no!   Let me shelter you!   Let me!

CLARE. [*Shaking her head and smiling*] I'm going to seek my fortune.   Wish me luck!

MALISE. I *can't* let you go.

CLARE. You *must*.

> *He looks into her face; then, realizing that she
> means it, suddenly bends down to her fingers,
> and puts his lips to them.*

MALISE. Good luck, then! Good luck!

> *He releases her hand. Just touching his bent
> head with her other hand, CLARE turns and
> goes. MALISE remains with bowed head, listen-
> ing to the sound of her receding footsteps. They
> die away. He raises himself, and strikes out
> into the air with his clenched fist.*

CURTAIN.

ACT III

MALISE's *sitting-room. An afternoon, three months later. On the table are an open bottle of claret, his hat, and some tea-things. Down in the hearth is a kettle on a lighted spirit-stand. Near the door stands* HAYWOOD, *a short, round-faced man, with a tobacco-coloured moustache;* MALISE, *by the table, is contemplating a piece of blue paper.*

HAYWOOD. Sorry to press an old customer, sir, but a year and an 'alf without any return on your money——

MALISE. Your tobacco is too good, Mr. Haywood. I wish I could see my way to smoking another.

HAYWOOD. Well, sir—that's a funny remedy.

With a knock on the half-opened door, a BOY *appears.*

MALISE. Yes. What is it?

BOY. Your copy for "The Watchfire," please, sir.

MALISE. [*Motioning him out*] Yes. Wait!

The BOY *withdraws.* MALISE *goes up to the pile of books, turns them over, and takes up some volumes.*

MALISE. This is a very fine unexpurgated translation of Boccaccio's "Decameron," Mr. Haywood—illustrated. I should say you would get more than the amount of your bill for them.

51

HAYWOOD. [*Shaking his head*] Them books worth three pound seven!

MALISE. It's scarce, and highly improper. Will you take them in discharge?

HAYWOOD. [*Torn between emotions*] Well, I 'ardly know what to say— No, sir, I don't think I'd like to 'ave to do with that.

MALISE. You could read them first, you know?

HAYWOOD. [*Dubiously*] I've got my wife at 'ome.

MALISE. You could both read them.

HAYWOOD. [*Brought to his bearings*] No, sir, I couldn't.

MALISE. Very well; I'll sell them myself, and you shall have the result.

HAYWOOD. Well, thank you, sir. I'm sure I didn't want to trouble you.

MALISE. Not at all, Mr. Haywood. It's for me to apologize.

HAYWOOD. So long as I give satisfaction.

MALISE. [*Holding the door for him*] Certainly. Good evening.

HAYWOOD. Good evenin', sir; no offence, I hope.

MALISE. On the contrary.

> *Doubtfully* HAYWOOD *goes. And* MALISE *stands scratching his head; then slipping the bill into one of the volumes to remind him, he replaces them at the top of the pile. The* BOY *again advances into the doorway.*

MALISE. Yes, now for you.

> *He goes to the table and takes some sheets of MS.*

from an old portfolio. But the door is again
timidly pushed open, and HAYWOOD *reappears.*

MALISE. Yes, Mr. Haywood?

HAYWOOD. About that little matter, sir. If—if it's
any convenience to you—I've—thought of a place
where I could——

MALISE. Read them? You'll enjoy them thor-
oughly.

HAYWOOD, No, sir, no! Where I can dispose of
them.

MALISE. [*Holding out the volumes*] It might be as
well. [HAYWOOD *takes the books gingerly*] I congratu-
late you, Mr. Haywood; it's a classic.

HAYWOOD. Oh, indeed—yes, sir. In the event of
there being any——

MALISE. Anything over? Carry it to my credit.
Your bill—— [*He hands over the blue paper*] Send me
the receipt.   Good evening!

> HAYWOOD, *nonplussed, and trying to hide the*
> *books in an evening paper, fumbles out :* "Good
> evenin', sir!" *and departs.* MALISE *again*
> *takes up the sheets of MS. and cons a sentence*
> *over to himself, gazing blankly at the stolid*
> BOY.

MALISE. "Man of the world—good form your god!
Poor buttoned-up philosopher" [*the* BOY *shifts his feet*]
"inbred to the point of cretinism, and founded to the
bone on fear of ridicule [*the* BOY *breathes heavily*]—you
are the slave of facts!"

> [*There is a knock on the door.*

MALISE. Who is it?

The door is pushed open, and REGINALD HUNT-
INGDON *stands there.*

HUNTINGDON. I apologize, sir; can I come in a
minute?

[MALISE *bows with ironical hostility.*

HUNTINGDON. I don't know if you remember me—
Clare Dedmond's brother.

MALISE. I remember you.

[*He motions to the stolid* BOY *to go outside again.*

HUNTINGDON. I've come to you, sir, as a gentleman——

MALISE. Some mistake. There is one, I believe, on
the first floor.

HUNTINGDON. It's about my sister.

MALISE. D—n you! Don't you know that I've
been shadowed these last three months? Ask your
detectives for any information you want.

HUNTINGDON. We know that you haven't seen her,
or even known where she is.

MALISE. Indeed! You've found that out? Bril-
liant!

HUNTINGDON. We know it from my sister.

MALISE. Oh! So you've tracked her down?

HUNTINGDON. Mrs. Fullarton came across her yesterday in one of those big shops—selling gloves.

MALISE. Mrs. Fullarton—the lady with the husband.
Well! you've got her. Clap her back into prison.

HUNTINGDON. We have not got her. She left at
once, and we don't know where she's gone.

MALISE. Bravo!

HUNTINGDON. [*Taking hold of his bit*] Look here, Mr. Malise, in a way I share your feeling, but I'm fond of my sister, and it's damnable to have to go back to India knowing she must be all adrift, without protection, going through God knows what! Mrs. Fullarton says she's looking awfully pale and down.

MALISE. [*Struggling between resentment and sympathy*] Why do you come to me?

HUNTINGDON. We thought——

MALISE. *Who?*

HUNTINGDON. My—my father and myself.

MALISE. Go on.

HUNTINGDON. We thought there was just a chance that, having lost that job, she might come to you again for advice. If she does, it would be really generous of you if you'd put my father in touch with her. He's getting old, and he feels this very much. [*He hands* MALISE *a card*] This is his address.

MALISE. [*Twisting the card*] Let there be no mistake, sir; I do nothing that will help give her back to her husband. She's out to save her soul alive, and I don't join the hue and cry that's after her. On the contrary —if I had the power. If your father wants to shelter her, that's another matter. But she'd her own ideas about that.

HUNTINGDON. Perhaps you don't realize how unfit my sister is for rough and tumble. She's not one of this new sort of woman. She's always been looked after, and had things done for her.   Pluck she's got, but that's all, and she's bound to come to grief.

MALISE. Very likely—the first birds do.   But if she drops half-way it's better than if she'd never flown. Your sister, sir, is trying the wings of her spirit, out of the old slave market.   For women as for men, there's more than one kind of dishonour, Captain Huntingdon, and worse things than being dead, as you may know in your profession.

HUNTINGDON. Admitted—but——

MALISE. We each have our own views as to what they are.   But they all come to—death of our spirits, for the sake of our carcases.   Anything more?

HUNTINGDON. My leave's up.   I sail to-morrow.   If you do see my sister I trust you to give her my love and say I begged she would see my father.

MALISE. If I have the chance—yes.

> He makes a gesture of salute, to which HUNTING-
> DON responds.   Then the latter turns and goes
> out.

MALISE. Poor fugitive!   Where are you running now?

> He stands at the window, through which the even-
> ing sunlight is powdering the room with smoky
> gold.   The stolid BOY has again come in.   MA-
> LISE stares at him, then goes back to the table,
> takes up the MS., and booms it at him; he re-
> ceives the charge, breathing hard.

MALISE. "Man of the world—product of a material age; incapable of perceiving reality in motions of the spirit; having 'no use,' as you would say, for 'senti-

mental nonesnse'; accustomed to believe yourself the
national spine—your position is unassailable.   You will
remain the idol of the country—arbiter of law, parson
in mufti, darling of the playwright and the novelist
—God bless you!—while waters lap these shores."

> *He places the sheets of MS. in an envelope, and
> hands them to the* BOY.

MALISE. You're going straight back to "The Watchfire"?

BOY. [*Stolidly*] Yes, sir.

MALISE. [*Staring at him*] You're a masterpiece.
D'you know that?

BOY. No, sir.

MALISE. Get out, then.

> *He lifts the portfolio from the table, and takes it
> into the inner room.   The* BOY, *putting his
> thumb stolidly to his nose, turns to go.   In the
> doorway he shies violently at the figure of* CLARE,
> *standing there in a dark-coloured dress, skids
> past her and goes.   CLARE comes into the gleam
> of sunlight, her white face alive with emotion
> or excitement.   She looks round her, smiles,
> sighs; goes swiftly to the door, closes it, and
> comes back to the table.   There she stands, fin-
> gering the papers on the table, smoothing MA-
> LISE's hat—wistfully, eagerly, waiting.*

MALISE. [*Returning*] You!

CLARE. [*With a faint smile*] Not very glorious, is it?

> *He goes towards her, and checks himself, then
> slews the armchair round.*

MALISE. Come! Sit down, sit down! [CLARE, *heaving a long sigh, sinks down into the chair*] Tea's nearly ready.

> *He places a cushion for her, and prepares tea; she looks up at him softly, but as he finishes and turns to her, she drops that glance.*

CLARE. Do you think me an awful coward for coming? [*She has taken a little plain cigarette case from her dress*] Would you mind if I smoked?

> MALISE *shakes his head, then draws back from her again, as if afraid to be too close. And again, unseen, she looks at him.*

MALISE. So you've lost your job?

CLARE. How did you——?

MALISE. Your brother. You only just missed him. [CLARE *starts up*] They had an idea you'd come. He's sailing to-morrow—he wants you to see your father.

CLARE. Is father ill?

MALISE. Anxious about you.

CLARE. I've written to him every week. [*Excited*] They're still hunting me!

MALISE. [*Touching her shoulder gently*] It's all right —all right.

> *She sinks again into the chair, and again he withdraws. And once more she gives him that soft eager look, and once more averts it as he turns to her.*

CLARE. My nerves have gone funny lately. It's being always on one's guard, and stuffy air, and feeling people look and talk about you, and dislike your being there.

MALISE. Yes; that wants pluck.

CLARE. [*Shaking her head*] I curl up all the time. The only thing I know for certain is, that I shall never go back to him. The more I've hated what I've been doing, the more sure I've been. I might come to any-thing—but not that.

MALISE. Had a very bad time?

CLARE. [*Nodding*] I'm spoilt. It's a curse to be a lady when you have to earn your living. It's not really been so hard, I suppose; I've been selling things, and living about twice as well as most shop girls.

MALISE. Were they decent to you?

CLARE. Lots of the girls are really nice. But some-how they don't want me, can't help thinking I've got airs or something; and in here [*She touches her breast*] I don't want them!

MALISE. I know.

CLARE. Mrs. Fullarton and I used to belong to a society for helping reduced gentlewomen to get work. I know now what they want: enough money *not* to work—that's all! [*Suddenly looking up at him*] Don't think me worse than I am—please! It's working *un-der* people; it's *having* to do it, being driven. I *have* tried, I've not been altogether a coward, really! But every morning getting there the same time; every day the same stale "dinner," as they call it; every evening the same "Good evening, Miss Clare," "Good evening, Miss Simpson," "Good evening, Miss Hart," "Good evening, Miss Clare." And the same walk home, or the same 'bus; and the same men that you mustn't look at, for fear they'll follow you. [*She rises*] Oh! and the feeling—always, always—that there's no sun, or life, or hope, or anything. It was just like being ill, the way I've wanted to ride and dance and get out into the country. [*Her excitement dies away into the old clipped composure, and she sits down again*] Don't think too badly of me—it really is pretty ghastly!

MALISE. [*Gruffly*] H'm! Why a shop?

CLARE. References. I didn't want to tell more lies than I could help; a married woman on strike can't tell the truth, you know. And I can't typewrite or do shorthand yet. And chorus—I thought—*you* wouldn't like.

MALISE. I? What have I——? [*He checks himself*] Have men been brutes?

CLARE. [*Stealing a look at him*] One followed me a lot. He caught hold of my arm one evening. I just took this out [*She draws out her hatpin and holds it like a dagger, her lip drawn back as the lips of a dog going to bite*] and said: "Will you leave me alone, please?" And he did. It was rather nice. And there was one quite decent little man in the shop—I was sorry for *him*—such a humble little man!

MALISE. Poor devil—it's hard not to wish for the moon.

> *At the tone of his voice* CLARE *looks up at him;*
> *his face is turned away.*

CLARE. [*Softly*] How have *you* been? Working very hard?

MALISE. As hard as God will let me.

CLARE. [*Stealing another look*] Have you any type-writing I could do? I could learn, and I've still got a brooch I could sell. Which is the best kind?

MALISE. I had a catalogue of them somewhere.

> *He goes into the inner room. The moment he is gone, CLARE stands up, her hands pressed to her cheeks as if she felt them flaming. Then, with hands clasped, she stands waiting. He comes back with the old portfolio.*

MALISE. Can you typewrite where you are?

CLARE. I have to find a new room anyway. I'm changing—to be safe. [*She takes a luggage ticket from her glove*] I took my things to Charing Cross—only a bag and one trunk. [*Then, with that queer expression on her face which prefaces her desperations*] You don't want me now, I suppose.

MALISE. What?

CLARE. [*Hardly above a whisper*] Because—if you still wanted me—I do—now.

MALISE. [*Staring hard into her face that is quivering and smiling*] You mean it? You *do*? You care——?

CLARE. I've thought of you—so much! But only—if you're sure.

> *He clasps her and kisses her closed eyes; and so they stand for a moment, till the sound of a latchkey in the door sends them apart.*

MALISE. It's the housekeeper. Give me that ticket; I'll send for your things.

> *Obediently she gives him the ticket, smiles, and goes quietly into the inner room.* MRS. MILER

has entered ; her face, more Chinese than ever, shows no sign of having seen.

MALISE. That lady will stay here, Mrs. Miler. Kindly go with this ticket to the cloak-room at Charing Cross station, and bring back her luggage in a cab. Have you money?

MRS. MILER. 'Arf a crown. [*She takes the ticket— then impassively*] In case you don't know—there's two o' them men about the stairs now.

> *The moment she is gone* MALISE *makes a gesture of maniacal fury. He steals on tiptoe to the outer door, and listens. Then, placing his hand on the knob, he turns it without noise, and wrenches back the door. Transfigured in the last sunlight streaming down the corridor are two men, close together, listening and consulting secretly. They start back.*

MALISE. [*With strange, almost noiseless ferocity*] You've run her to earth; your job's done. Kennel up, hounds!   [*And in their faces he slams the door.*

CURTAIN.

SCENE II

SCENE II.—*The same, early on a winter afternoon, three
months later. The room has now a certain dainti-
ness. There are curtains over the doors, a couch
under the window, all the books are arranged on
shelves. In small vases, over the fireplace, are a
few violets and chrysanthemums.* MALISE *sits hud-
dled in his armchair drawn close to the fire, paper
on knee, pen in hand. He looks rather grey and
drawn, and round his chair is the usual litter. At
the table, now nearer to the window,* CLARE *sits
working a typewriter. She finishes a line, puts
sheets of paper together, makes a note on a card—
adds some figures, and marks the total.*

CLARE. Kenneth, when this is paid, I shall have
made two pound seventeen in the three months, and
saved you about three pounds. One hundred and
seventeen shillings at tenpence a thousand is one
hundred and forty thousand words at fourteen hundred
words an hour. It's only just over an hour a day.
Can't you get me more?

> MALISE *lifts the hand that holds his pen and lets
> it fall again.* CLARE *puts the cover on the type-
> writer, and straps it.*

CLARE. I'm quite packed. Shall I pack for you?
[*He nods*] Can't we have more than three days at the
sea? [*He shakes his head. Going up to him*] You *did*
sleep last night.

MALISE. Yes, I slept.

CLARE. Bad head? [MALISE *nods*] By this time the day after to-morrow the case will be heard and done with. You're not worrying for me? Except for my poor old Dad, *I* don't care a bit.

> MALISE *heaves himself out of the chair, and begins pacing up and down.*

CLARE. Kenneth, do you understand why he doesn't claim damages, after what he said that day—here? [*Looking suddenly at him*] It *is* true that he doesn't?

MALISE. It is not.

CLARE. But you told me yourself——

MALISE. I lied.

CLARE. Why?

MALISE. [*Shrugging*] No use lying any longer— you'd know it to-morrow.

CLARE. How much am I valued at?

MALISE. Two thousand. [*Grimly*] He'll settle it on you. [*He laughs*] Masterly! By one stroke, destroys his enemy, avenges his "honour," and gilds his name with generosity!

CLARE. Will you *have* to pay?

MALISE. Stones yield no blood.

CLARE. Can't you borrow?

MALISE. I couldn't even get the costs.

CLARE. Will they make you bankrupt, then? [MALISE *nods*] But that doesn't mean that you won't have your *income*, does it? [MALISE *laughs*] What is your income, Kenneth? [*He is silent*] A hundred and fifty from "The Watchfire," I know. What else?

MALISE. Out of five books I have made the sum of forty pounds.

CLARE. What else? Tell me.

MALISE. Fifty to a hundred pounds a year. Leave me to gnaw my way out, child.

> CLARE *stands looking at him in distress, then goes quickly into the room behind her.* MALISE *takes up his paper and pen. The paper is quite blank.*

MALISE. [*Feeling his head*] Full of smoke.

> *He drops paper and pen, and crossing to the room on the left goes in.* CLARE *re-enters with a small leather box. She puts it down on her typing table as* MALISE *returns followed by* MRS. MILER, *wearing her hat, and carrying his overcoat.*

MRS. MILER. Put your coat on. It's a bitter wind.
> [*He puts on the coat.*

CLARE. Where are you going?

MALISE. To "The Watchfire."

> *The door closes behind him, and* MRS. MILER *goes up to* CLARE *holding out a little blue bottle with a red label, nearly full.*

MRS. MILER. You know he's takin' this [*She makes a little motion towards her mouth*] to make 'im sleep?

CLARE. [*Reading the label*] Where was it?

MRS. MILER. In the bathroom chest o' drawers, where 'e keeps 'is odds and ends. I was lookin' for 'is garters.

CLARE. Give it to me!

Mrs. Miler. He took it once before. He must get his sleep.

Clare. Give it to me!

> Mrs. Miler *resigns it,* Clare *takes the cork out, smells, then tastes it from her finger.* Mrs. Miler, *twisting her apron in her hands, speaks.*

Mrs. Miler. I've 'ad it on my mind a long time to speak to yer. Your comin' 'ere's not done 'im a bit o' good.

Clare. Don't!

Mrs. Miler. I don't want to, but what with the worry o' this 'ere divorce suit, an' you bein' a lady an' 'im havin' to be so careful of yer, and tryin' to save, not smokin' all day like 'e used, an' not gettin' 'is two bottles of claret regular; an' losin' his sleep, an' takin' that stuff for it; and now this 'ere last business. I've seen 'im sometimes holdin' 'is 'ead as if it was comin' off. [*Seeing* Clare *wince, she goes on with a sort of compassion in her Chinese face*] I can see yer fond of him; an' I've nothin' against yer—you don't trouble me a bit; but I've been with 'im eight years—we're used to each other, and I can't bear to see 'im not 'imself, really I can't.

> She gives a sudden sniff.   Then her emotion passes, leaving her as Chinese as ever.

Clare. This last business—what do you mean by that?

Mrs. Miler. If 'e a'n't told yer, I don't know that I've any call to.

Clare. Please.

MRS. MILER. [*Her hands twisting very fast*] Well, it's to do with this 'ere "Watchfire." One of the men that sees to the writin' of it—'e's an old friend of Mr. Malise, 'e come 'ere this mornin' when you was out. I was doin' my work in there [*She points to the room on the right*] an' the door open, so I 'eard 'em. Now you've 'ung them curtains, you can't 'elp it.

CLARE. Yes?

MRS. MILER. It's about your divorce case. This 'ere "Watchfire," ye see, belongs to some fellers that won't 'ave their men gettin' into the papers. So this 'ere friend of Mr. Malise—very nice 'e spoke about it—"If it comes into Court," 'e says, "you'll 'ave to go," 'e says. "These beggars, these dogs, these logs," 'e says, "they'll 'oof you out," 'e says. An' I could tell by the sound of his voice, 'e meant it—proper upset 'e was. So that's that!

CLARE. It's inhuman!

MRS. MILER. That's what I thinks; but it don't 'elp, do it? "'Tain't the circulation," 'e says, "it's the principle," 'e says; and then 'e starts in swearin' horrible. 'E's a very nice man. And Mr. Malise, 'e says: "Well, that about does for me!" 'e says.

CLARE. Thank you, Mrs. Miler—I'm glad to know.

MRS. MILER. Yes; I don't know as I ought to 'ave told you. [*Desperately uncomfortable*] You see, I don't take notice of Mr. Malise, but I know 'im very well. 'E's a good-'earted gentleman, very funny, that'll do things to help others, and what's more, keep on doin' 'em, when they hurt 'im; very obstinate 'e is. Now, when you first come 'ere, three months ago, I says to meself: "He'll enjoy this 'ere for a bit, but she's too much of a lady for 'im." What 'e wants about 'im permanent is a woman that thinks an' talks about all them things he talks about. And sometimes I fancy 'e don't want nothin' permanent about 'im at all.

CLARE. Don't!

MRS. MILER. [*With another sudden sniff*] Gawd knows I don't want to upset ye. You're situated very 'ard; an' women's got no business to 'urt one another —that's what I thinks.

CLARE. Will you go out and do something for me? [MRS. MILER *nods.* CLARE *takes up the sheaf of papers and from the leather box a note and an emerald pendant*] Take this with the note to that address—it's quite close. He'll give you thirty pounds for it. Please pay these bills and bring me back the receipts, and what's over.

MRS. MILER. [*Taking the pendant and note*] It's a pretty thing.

CLARE. Yes. It was my mother's.

MRS. MILER. It's a pity to part with it; ain't you got another?

CLARE. Nothing more, Mrs. Miler, not even a wedding ring.

MRS. MILER. [*Without expression*] You make my 'eart ache sometimes.

> *She wraps pendant and note into her handkerchief and goes out to the door.*

MRS. MILER. [*From the door*] There's a lady and

gentleman out here. Mrs. Fuller—wants *you*, not Mr. Malise.

CLARE. Mrs. Fullarton? [MRS. MILER *nods*] Ask them to come in.

> MRS. MILER *opens the door wide, says* "Come in," *and goes.* MRS. FULLARTON *is accompanied not by* FULLARTON, *but by the lawyer,* TWISDEN. *They come in.*

MRS. FULLARTON. Clare! My dear! How are you after all this time?

CLARE. [*Her eyes fixed on* TWISDEN] Yes?

MRS. FULLARTON. [*Disconcerted by the strange greeting*] I brought Mr. Twisden to tell you something. May I stay?

CLARE. Yes. [*She points to the chair at the same table:* MRS. FULLARTON *sits down*] Now!

> [TWISDEN *comes forward.*

TWISDEN. As you're not defending this case, Mrs. Dedmond, there is nobody but yourself for me to apply to.

CLARE. Please tell me quickly, what you've come for.

TWISDEN. [*Bowing slightly*] I am instructed by Mr. Dedmond to say that if you will leave your present companion and undertake not to see him again, he will withdraw the suit and settle three hundred a year on you. [*At* CLARE'S *movement of abhorrence*] Don't misunderstand me, please—it is not—it could hardly be, a request that you should go back. Mr. Dedmond is *not* prepared to receive you again. The proposal—forgive my saying so—remarkably Quixotic

—is made to save the scandal to his family and your own. It binds you to nothing but the abandonment of your present companion, with certain conditions of the same nature as to the future. In other words, it assures you a position—so long as you live quietly by yourself.

CLARE. I see. Will you please thank Mr. Dedmond, and say that I refuse?

MRS. FULLARTON. Clare, Clare! For God's sake don't be desperate.

[CLARE, *deathly still, just looks at her.*

TWISDEN. Mrs. Dedmond, I am bound to put the position to you in its naked brutality. You know there's a claim for damages?

CLARE. I have just learnt it.

TWISDEN. You realize what the result of this suit must be: You will be left dependent on an undischarged bankrupt. To put it another way, you'll be a stone round the neck of a drowning man.

CLARE. You are cowards.

MRS. FULLARTON. Clare, Clare! [*To* TWISDEN] She doesn't mean it; *please* be patient.

CLARE. I *do* mean it. You ruin him because of me. You get him down, and kick him to intimidate me.

MRS. FULLARTON. My dear girl! Mr. Twisden is not personally concerned. How can you?

CLARE. If I were dying, and it would save me, I wouldn't take a penny from my husband.

TWISDEN. Nothing could be more bitter than those

words. Do you really wish me to take them back to him?

CLARE. Yes.   [*She turns from them to the fire.*

MRS. FULLARTON. [*In a low voice to* TWISDEN] Please leave me alone with her, don't say anything to Mr. Dedmond yet.

TWISDEN. Mrs. Dedmond, I told you once that I wished you well. Though you have called me a coward, I still do that. For God's sake, think—before it's too late.

CLARE. [*Putting out her hand blindly*] I'm sorry I called you a coward. It's the whole thing, I meant.

TWISDEN. Never mind that. Think!

> *With the curious little movement of one who sees something he does not like to see, he goes.* CLARE *is leaning her forehead against the mantelshelf, seemingly unconscious that she is not alone.* MRS. FULLARTON *approaches quietly till she can see* CLARE'S *face.*

MRS. FULLARTON. My dear sweet thing, don't be cross with *me!* [CLARE *turns from her. It is all the time as if she were trying to get away from words and people to something going on within herself*] How can I help wanting to see you saved from all this ghastliness?

CLARE. Please don't, Dolly! Let me be!

MRS. FULLARTON. I must speak, Clare! I do think you're hard on George. It's generous of him to offer to withdraw the suit—considering. You do owe it to us to try and spare your father and your sisters and—and all of us who care for you.

CLARE. [*Facing her*] You say George is generous! If he wanted to be that he'd never have claimed those damages. It's revenge he wants—I heard him here. You think I've done him an injury. So I did—when I married him. I don't know what I shall come to, Dolly, but I shan't fall so low as to take money from him. That's as certain as that I shall die.

MRS. FULLARTON. Do you know, Clare, I think it's awful about you! You're too fine, and not fine enough, to put up with things; you're too sensitive to take help, and you're not strong enough to do without it. It's simply tragic. At any rate, you might go home to your people.

CLARE. After *this!*

MRS. FULLARTON. To us, then?

CLARE. "If I could be the falling bee, and kiss thee all the day!" No, Dolly!

> MRS. FULLARTON *turns from her ashamed and baffled, but her quick eyes take in the room, trying to seize on some new point of attack.*

MRS. FULLARTON. You can't be—you aren't—happy, here ?

CLARE. Aren't I ?

MRS. FULLARTON. Oh! Clare! Save yourself—and all of us!

CLARE. [*Very still*] You see, I love him.

MRS. FULLARTON. You used to say you'd never love; did not want it—would never want it.

CLARE. Did I ? How funny!

Mrs. Fullarton. Oh! my dear! Don't look like that, or you'll make me cry.

Clare. One doesn't always know the future, does one? [*Desperately*] I love him! I love him!

Mrs. Fullarton. [*Suddenly*] If you love him, what will it be like for you, knowing you've ruined him?

Clare. Go away! Go away!

Mrs. Fullarton. Love!—you said!

Clare. [*Quivering at that stab—suddenly*] I must— I will keep him. He's all I've got.

Mrs. Fullarton. Can you—*can* you keep him?

Clare. Go!

Mrs. Fullarton. I'm going. But, men are hard to keep, even when you've not been the ruin of them. You know whether the love this man gives you is really love. If not—God help you! [*She turns at the door, and says mournfully*] Good-bye, my child! If you can——

> *Then goes.* Clare, *almost in a whisper, repeats the words:* "Love! you said!" *At the sound of a latchkey she runs as if to escape into the bedroom, but changes her mind and stands blotted against the curtain of the door.* Malise *enters. For a moment he does not see her standing there against the curtain that is much the same colour as her dress. His face is that of a man in the grip of a rage that he feels to be impotent. Then, seeing her, he pulls himself together, walks to his armchair, and sits down there in his hat and coat.*

CLARE. Well? "The Watchfire?" You may as well tell me.

MALISE. Nothing to tell you, child.

At that touch of tenderness she goes up to his chair and kneels down beside it. Mechanically MALISE takes off his hat.

CLARE. Then you are to lose that, too? [MALISE *stares at her*] I know about it—never mind how.

MALISE. Sanctimonious dogs!

CLARE. [*Very low*] There are other things to be got, aren't there?

MALISE. Thick as blackberries. I just go out and cry, "Malise, unsuccessful author, too honest journalist, freethinker, co-respondent, bankrupt," and they tumble!

CLARE. [*Quietly*] Kenneth, do you care for me? [MALISE *stares at her*] Am I anything to you but just prettiness?

MALISE. Now, now! This isn't the time to brood! Rouse up and fight.

CLARE. Yes.

MALISE. We're not going to let them down us, are we? [*She rubs her cheek against his hand, that still rests on her shoulder*] Life on sufferance, breath at the pleasure of the enemy! And some day in the fullness of his mercy to be made a present of the right to eat and drink and breathe again. [*His gesture sums up the rage within him*] Fine! [*He puts his hat on and rises*] That's the last groan they get from me.

CLARE. Are you going out again? [*He nods*] Where?

MALISE. Blackberrying! Our train's not till six.

He goes into the bedroom. CLARE gets up and stands by the fire, looking round in a dazed way. She puts her hand up and mechanically gathers together the violets in the little vase. Suddenly she twists them to a button-hole, and sinks down into the armchair, which he must pass. There she sits, the violets in her hand. MALISE comes out and crosses towards the outer door. She puts the violets up to him. He stares at them, shrugs his shoulders, and passes on. For just a moment CLARE sits motionless.

CLARE. [*Quietly*] Give me a kiss!

He turns and kisses her. But his lips, after that kiss, have the furtive bitterness one sees on the lips of those who have done what does not suit their mood. He goes out. She is left motionless by the armchair, her throat working. Then, feverishly, she goes to the little table, seizes a sheet of paper, and writes. Looking up suddenly she sees that MRS. MILER has let herself in with her latchkey.

MRS. MILER. I've settled the baker, the milk, the washin' an' the groceries—this 'ere's what's left.

She counts down a five-pound note, four sovereigns, and two shillings on to the little table. CLARE folds the letter into an envelope, then takes up the five-pound note and puts it into her dress.

CLARE. [*Pointing to the money on the table*] Take

your wages; and give him this when he comes in. I'm going away.

MRS. MILER. Without him? When'll you be comin' back?

CLARE. [*Rising*] I shan't be coming back. [*Gazing at* MRS. MILER's *hands, which are plaiting at her dress*] I'm leaving Mr. Malise, and shan't see him again. And the suit against us will be withdrawn—the divorce suit—you understand?

MRS. MILER. [*Her face all broken up*] I never meant to say anything to yer.

CLARE. It's not you. I can see for myself. Don't make it harder; help me. Get a cab.

MRS. MILER. [*Disturbed to the heart*] The porter's outside, cleanin' the landin' winder.

CLARE. Tell him to come for my trunk. It is packed.   [*She goes into the bedroom.*

MRS. MILER. [*Opening the door—desolately*] Come 'ere!

      [*The* PORTER *appears in shirt-sleeves at the door.*

MRS. MILER. The lady wants a cab. Wait and carry 'er trunk down.

      CLARE *comes from the bedroom in her hat and coat.*

MRS. MILER. [*To the* PORTER] Now.

      They go into the bedroom to get the trunk. CLARE
      *picks up from the floor the bunch of violets, her
      fingers play with it as if they did not quite know
      what it was; and she stands by the armchair very
      still, while* MRS. MILER *and the* PORTER *pass*

her with trunk and bag. And even after the
PORTER *has shouldered the trunk outside, and
marched away, and* MRS. MILER *has come back
into the room,* CLARE *still stands there.*

MRS. MILER. [*Pointing to the typewriter*] D'you want
this 'ere, too?

CLARE. Yes.

MRS. MILER *carries it out. Then, from the doorway, gazing at* CLARE *taking her last look, she
sobs, suddenly. At sound of that sob* CLARE
throws up her head.

CLARE. Don't! It's all right. Good-bye!

She walks out and away, not looking back. MRS.
MILER *chokes her sobbing into the black stuff
of her thick old jacket.*

CURTAIN.

ACT IV

SUPPER-TIME *in a small room at "The Gascony" on
Derby Day. Through the windows of a broad
corridor, out of which the door opens, is seen the
dark blue of a summer night. The walls are of
apricot-gold; the carpets, curtains, lamp-shades,
and gilded chairs, of red; the wood-work and screens
white; the palms in gilded tubs. A doorway that
has no door leads to another small room. One
little table behind a screen, and one little table in
the open, are set for two persons each. On a service-table, above which hangs a speaking-tube, are
some dishes of hors d'œuvres, a basket of peaches,
two bottles of champagne in ice-pails, and a small
barrel of oysters in a gilded tub.* ARNAUD, *the
waiter, slim, dark, quick, his face seamed with a
quiet, soft irony, is opening oysters and listening
to the robust joy of a distant supper-party, where a
man is playing the last bars of:* "Do ye ken John
Peel" *on a horn. As the sound dies away, he
murmurs:* "Très Joli!" *and opens another oyster.
Two Ladies with bare shoulders and large hats pass
down the corridor. Their talk is faintly wafted in:*
"Well, I never like Derby night! The boys do
get so bobbish!" "That horn—vulgar, I call it!"

> ARNAUD'S *eyebrows rise, the corners of his mouth droop. A Lady with bare shoulders, and crimson roses in her hair, comes along the corridor, and stops for a second at the window, for a man to join her. They come through into the room.* ARNAUD *has sprung to attention, but with:* "Let's go in here, shall we?" *they pass through into the further room. The* MANAGER, *a gentleman with neat moustaches, and buttoned into a frock-coat, has appeared, brisk, noiseless, his eyes everywhere; he inspects the peaches.*

MANAGER. Four shillin' apiece to-night, see?

ARNAUD. Yes, Sare.

> *From the inner room a young man and his partner have come in. She is dark, almost Spanish-looking; he fair, languid, pale, clean-shaved, slackly smiling, with half-closed eyes—one of those who are bred and dissipated to the point of having lost all save the capacity for hiding their emotions. He speaks in a—*

LANGUID VOICE. Awful row they're kickin' up in there, Mr. Varley. A fellow with a horn.

MANAGER. [*Blandly*] Gaddesdon Hunt, my lord—always have their supper with us, Derby night. Quiet corner here, my lord. Arnaud!

> ARNAUD *is already at the table, between screen and palm. And, there ensconced, the couple take their seats. Seeing them safely landed, the* MANAGER, *brisk and noiseless, moves away. In the corridor a lady in black, with a cloak fall-*

> *ing open, seems uncertain whether to come in.*
> *She advances into the doorway. It is* CLARE.

ARNAUD. [*Pointing to the other table as he flies with dishes*] Nice table, Madame.

> CLARE *moves to the corner of it. An artist in*
> *observation of his clients,* ARNAUD *takes in*
> *her face—very pale under her wavy, simply-*
> *dressed hair; shadowy beneath the eyes; not*
> *powdered; her lips not reddened; without a sin-*
> *gle ornament; takes in her black dress, finely*
> *cut, her arms and neck beautifully white, and*
> *at her breast three gardenias. And as he nears*
> *her, she lifts her eyes. It is very much the look*
> *of something lost, appealing for guidance.*

ARNAUD. Madame is waiting for some one? [*She shakes her head*] Then Madame will be veree well here— veree well. I take Madame's cloak?

> *He takes the cloak gently and lays it on the back of*
> *the chair fronting the room, that she may put it*
> *round her when she wishes. She sits down.*

LANGUID VOICE. [*From the corner*] Waiter!

ARNAUD. Milord!

LANGUID VOICE. The Roederer.

ARNAUD. At once, milord.

> CLARE *sits tracing a pattern with her finger on*
> *the cloth, her eyes lowered. Once she raises*
> *them, and follows* ARNAUD's *dark rapid figure.*

ARNAUD. [*Returning*] Madame feels the 'eat? [*He scans her with increased curiosity*] You wish something, Madame?

CLARE. [*Again giving him that look*] *Must* I order?

ARNAUD. Non, Madame, it is not necessary. A glass of water. [*He pours it out*] I have not the pleasure of knowing Madame's face.

CLARE. [*Faintly smiling*] No.

ARNAUD. Madame will find it veree good 'ere, veree quiet.

LANGUID VOICE. Waiter!

ARNAUD. Pardon!   [*He goes.*

> *The bare-necked ladies with large hats again pass down the corridor outside, and again their voices are wafted in:* "Tottie! Not she! Oh! my goodness, she has got a pride on her!" "Bobbie'll never stick it!" "Look here, dear——" *Galvanized by those sounds,* CLARE *has caught her cloak and half-risen; they die away and she subsides.*

ARNAUD. [*Back at her table, with a quaint shrug towards the corridor*] It is not rowdy here, Madame, as a rule—not as in some places. To-night a little noise. Madame is fond of flowers? [*He whisks out, and returns almost at once with a bowl of carnations from some table in the next room*] These smell good!

CLARE. You are very kind.

ARNAUD. [*With courtesy*] Not at all, Madame; a pleasure.   [*He bows.*

> *A young man, tall, thin, hard, straight, with close-cropped, sandyish hair and moustache, a face tanned very red, and one of those small, long, lean heads that only grow in Britain;*

*clad in a thin dark overcoat thrown open, an
opera hat pushed back, a white waistcoat round
his lean middle, he comes in from the corridor.
He looks round, glances at* CLARE, *passes her
table towards the further room, stops in the doorway, and looks back at her. Her eyes have just
been lifted, and are at once cast down again.
The young man wavers, catches* ARNAUD'S *eye,
jerks his head to summon him, and passes into
the further room.* ARNAUD *takes up the vase
that has been superseded, and follows him out.
And* CLARE *sits alone in silence, broken by the
murmurs of the languid lord and his partner,
behind the screen. She is breathing as if she
had been running hard. She lifts her eyes.
The tall young man, divested of hat and coat,
is standing by her table, holding out his hand
with a sort of bashful hardiness.*

YOUNG MAN. How d'you do? Didn't recognize you
at first. So sorry—awfully rude of me.

> CLARE'S *eyes seem to fly from him, to appeal to
> him, to resign herself all at once. Something in
> the* YOUNG MAN *responds. He drops his hand.*

CLARE. [*Faintly*] How d'you do?

YOUNG MAN. [*Stammering*] You—you been down
there to-day?

CLARE. Where?

YOUNG MAN. [*With a smile*] The Derby. What?
Don't you generally go down? [*He touches the other
chair*] May I?

CLARE. [*Almost in a whisper*] Yes.

> *As he sits down,* ARNAUD *returns and stands before them.*

ARNAUD. The plovers' eggs veree good to-night, Sare. Veree good, Madame. A peach or two, after. Veree good peaches. The Roederer, Sare—not bad at all. Madame likes it *frappé*, but not too cold—yes?

> [*He is away again to his service-table.*

YOUNG MAN. [*Burying his face in the carnations*] I say—these are jolly, aren't they? They do you pretty well here.

CLARE. Do they?

YOUNG MAN. You've never been here? [CLARE *shakes her head*] By Jove! I thought I didn't know your face. [CLARE *looks full at him. Again something moves in the* YOUNG MAN, *and he stammers*] I mean—not——

CLARE. It doesn't matter.

YOUNG MAN. [*Respectfully*] Of course, if I—if you were waiting for anybody, or anything—I——

> [*He half rises.*

CLARE. It's all right, thank you.

> *The* YOUNG MAN *sits down again, uncomfortable, nonplussed. There is silence, broken by the inaudible words of the languid lord, and the distant merriment of the supper-party.* ARNAUD *brings the plovers' eggs.*

YOUNG MAN. The wine, quick.

ARNAUD. At once, Sare.

YOUNG MAN. [*Abruptly*] Don't you ever go racing, then?

CLARE. No.

[ARNAUD *pours out champagne.*

YOUNG MAN. I remember awfully well my first day. It was pretty thick—lost every blessed bob, and my watch and chain, playin' three cards on the way home.

CLARE. Everything has a beginning, hasn't it?

[*She drinks. The* YOUNG MAN *stares at her.*

YOUNG MAN. [*Floundering in these waters deeper than he had bargained for*] I say—about things having beginnings—did you mean anything?

[CLARE *nods.*

YOUNG MAN. What! D'you mean it's really the first——?

CLARE *nods. The champagne has flicked her courage.*

YOUNG MAN. By George! [*He leans back*] I've often wondered.

ARNAUD. [*Again filling the glasses*] Monsieur finds——

YOUNG MAN. [*Abruptly*] It's all right.

He drains his glass, then sits bolt upright. Chivalry and the camaraderie of class have begun to stir in him.

YOUNG MAN. Of course I can see that you're not —I mean, that you're a—a lady. [CLARE *smiles*] And I say, you know—if you have to—because you're in a hole—I should feel a cad. Let me lend you——?

CLARE. [*Holding up her glass*] *Le vin est tiré, il faut le boire!*

> *She drinks. The French words, which he does not too well understand, completing his conviction that she is a lady, he remains quite silent, frowning. As* CLARE *held up her glass, two gentlemen have entered. The first is blond, of good height and a comely insolence. His crisp, fair hair, and fair brushed-up moustache are just going grey; an eyeglass is fixed in one of two eyes that lord it over every woman they see; his face is broad, and coloured with air and wine. His companion is a tall, thin, dark bird of the night, with sly, roving eyes, and hollow cheeks. They stand looking round, then pass into the further room; but in passing, they have stared unreservedly at* CLARE.

YOUNG MAN. [*Seeing her wince*] Look here! I'm afraid you must feel me rather a brute, you know.

CLARE. No, I don't; really.

YOUNG MAN. Are you absolute stoney? [CLARE *nods*] But [*Looking at her frock and cloak*] you're so awfully well——

CLARE. I had the sense to keep them.

YOUNG MAN. [*More and more disturbed*] I say, you know—I wish you'd let me lend you something. I had quite a good day down there.

CLARE. [*Again tracing her pattern on the cloth—then looking up at him full*] I can't take, for nothing.

YOUNG MAN. By Jove! I don't know—really, I

don't—this makes me feel pretty rotten. I mean, it's
your being a lady.

CLARE. [*Smiling*] That's not your fault, is it? You
see, I've been beaten all along the line. And I really
don't care what happens to me. [*She has that peculiar
fey look on her face now*] I really don't; except that I
don't take charity. It's lucky for me it's you, and not
some——

> *The supper-party is getting still more boisterous,
> and there comes a long view holloa, and a blast
> of the horn.*

YOUNG MAN. But I say, what about your people?
You must have people of some sort.

> *He is fast becoming fascinated, for her cheeks have
> begun to flush and her eyes to shine.*

CLARE. Oh, yes; I've had people, and a husband, and
—everything—— And here I am! Queer, isn't it?
[*She touches her glass*] This is going to my head! Do
you mind? I sha'n't sing songs and get up and dance,
and I won't cry, I promise you!

YOUNG MAN. [*Between fascination and chivalry*] By
George! One simply can't believe in this happening
to a lady——

CLARE. Have you got sisters? [*Breaking into her soft
laughter*] My brother's in India. I sha'n't meet *him*,
anyway.

YOUNG MAN. No, but—I say—are you really quite
cut off from everybody? [CLARE *nods*] Something
rather awful must have happened?

> *She smiles. The two gentlemen have returned.*

The blond one is again staring fixedly at CLARE. *This time she looks back at him, flaming; and, with a little laugh, he passes with his friend into the corridor.*

CLARE. Who are those two?

YOUNG MAN. Don't know—not been much about town yet. I'm just back from India myself. You said your brother was there; what's his regiment?

CLARE. [*Shaking her head*] You're not going to find out my name. I haven't got one—nothing.

She leans her bare elbows on the table, and her face on her hands.

CLARE. First of June! This day last year I broke covert—I've been running ever since.

YOUNG MAN. I don't understand a bit. You—must have had a—a—some one——

But there is such a change in her face, such rigidity of her whole body, that he stops and averts his eyes. When he looks again she is drinking. She puts the glass down, and gives a little laugh.

YOUNG MAN. [*With a sort of awe*] Anyway it must have been like riding at a pretty stiff fence, for you to come here to-night.

CLARE. Yes. What's the other side?

The YOUNG MAN *puts out his hand and touches her arm. It is meant for sympathy, but she takes it for attraction.*

CLARE. [*Shaking her head*] Not yet—please! I'm enjoying this. May I have a cigarette?

[*He takes out his case, and gives her one.*

CLARE. [*Letting the smoke slowly forth*] Yes, I'm enjoying it. Had a pretty poor time lately; not enough to eat, sometimes.

YOUNG MAN. Not really! How damnable! I say —do have something more substantial.

> CLARE *gives a sudden gasp, as if going off into hysterical laughter, but she stifles it, and shakes her head.*

YOUNG MAN. A peach?

> [ARNAUD *brings peaches to the table.*

CLARE. [*Smiling*] Thank you.

> [*He fills their glasses and retreats.*

CLARE. [*Raising her glass*] Eat and drink, for to-morrow we—Listen!

> *From the supper-party comes the sound of an abortive chorus:* "With a hey ho, chivy, hark forrard, hark forrard, tantivy!" *Jarring out into a discordant whoop, it sinks.*

CLARE. "This day a stag must die." Jolly old song!

YOUNG MAN. Rowdy lot! [*Suddenly*] I say—I admire your pluck.

CLARE. [*Shaking her head*] Haven't kept my end up. Lots of women do! You see: I'm too fine, and not fine enough! My best friend said that. Too fine, and not fine enough. [*She laughs*] I couldn't be a saint and martyr, and I wouldn't be a soulless doll. Neither one thing nor the other—that's the tragedy.

YOUNG MAN. You must have had awful luck!

CLARE. I *did* try. [*Fiercely*] But what's the good—when there's nothing before you?—Do I look ill?

YOUNG MAN. No; simply awfully pretty.

CLARE. [*With a laugh*] A man once said to me: "As you haven't money, you should never have been pretty!" But, you see, it is some good. If I hadn't been, I couldn't have risked coming here, could I? Don't you think it was rather sporting of me to buy these [*She touches the gardenias*] with the last shilling over from my cab fare?

YOUNG MAN. Did you really? D——d sporting!

CLARE. It's no use doing things by halves, is it? I'm—in for it—wish me luck! [*She drinks, and puts her glass down with a smile*] In for it—deep! [*She flings up her hands above her smiling face*] Down, down, till they're just above water, and then—down, down, down, and—all over! Are you sorry now you came and spoke to me?

YOUNG MAN. By Jove, no! It may be caddish, but I'm not.

CLARE. Thank God for beauty! I hope I shall die pretty! Do you think I shall *do* well?

YOUNG MAN. I say—*don't* talk like that!

CLARE. I want to know. *Do* you?

YOUNG MAN. Well, then—yes, I do.

CLARE. That's splendid. Those poor women in the streets would give their eyes, wouldn't they?—that have to go up and down, up and down! Do you think I—shall——

> The YOUNG MAN, *half-rising, puts his hand on her arm.*

YOUNG MAN. I think you're getting much too ex-

cited. You look all—Won't you eat your peach?
[*She shakes her head*] Do! Have something else, then
—some grapes, or something?

CLARE. No, thanks.

[*She has become quite calm again.*

YOUNG MAN. Well, then, what d'you think? It's
awfully hot in here, isn't it? Wouldn't it be jollier
drivin'? Shall we—shall we make a move?

CLARE. Yes.

The YOUNG MAN *turns to look for the waiter,
but* ARNAUD *is not in the room. He gets up.*

YOUNG MAN. [*Feverishly*] D——n that waiter! Wait
half a minute, if you don't mind, while I pay the bill.

*As he goes out into the corridor, the two gentlemen
re-appear.* CLARE *is sitting motionless, looking straight before her.*

DARK ONE. A fiver you don't get her to!

BLOND ONE. Done!

*He advances to her table with his inimitable inso-
lence, and taking the cigar from his mouth,
bends his stare on her, and says:* "Charmed to
see you lookin' so well! Will you have supper with me here to-morrow night?" *Startled
out of her reverie,* CLARE *looks up. She sees
those eyes, she sees beyond him the eyes of his
companion—sly, malevolent, amused—watching; and she just sits gazing, without a word.
At that regard, so clear, the* BLOND ONE *does not
wince. But rather suddenly he says:* "That's
arranged then. Half-past eleven. So good
of you. Good-night!" *He replaces his cigar*

*and strolls back to his companion, and in a low
voice says: "Pay up!" Then at a languid
"Hullo, Charles!" they turn to greet the two in
their nook behind the screen. CLARE has not
moved, nor changed the direction of her gaze.
Suddenly she thrusts her hand into the pocket
of the cloak that hangs behind her, and brings
out the little blue bottle which, six months ago,
she took from MALISE. She pulls out the cork
and pours the whole contents into her champagne.
She lifts the glass, holds it before her—smiling,
as if to call a toast, then puts it to her lips and
drinks. Still smiling, she sets the empty glass
down, and lays the gardenia flowers against
her face. Slowly she droops back in her chair,
the drowsy smile still on her lips; the gardenias
drop into her lap; her arms relax, her head falls
forward on her breast. And the voices behind
the screen talk on, and the sounds of joy from the
supper-party wax and wane.*

*The waiter, ARNAUD, returning from the corridor,
passes to his service-table with a tall, be-rib-
boned basket of fruit. Putting it down, he goes
towards the table behind the screen, and sees.
He runs up to CLARE.*

ARNAUD. Madame! Madame! [*He listens for her
breathing; then suddenly catching sight of the little bottle,
smells at it*] Bon Dieu!

> *At that queer sound they come from behind the screen
> —all four, and look. The dark night bird says:
> "Hallo; fainted!" ARNAUD holds out the bottle.*

LANGUID LORD. [*Taking it, and smelling*] Good God!
>   *The woman bends over* CLARE, *and lifts her hands;*
>   ARNAUD *rushes to his service-table, and speaks*
>   *into his tube:*

ARNAUD. The boss.   Quick! [*Looking up he sees the*
YOUNG MAN, *returning*] *Monsieur, elle a fui ! Elle est*
morte !

LANGUID LORD. [*To the* YOUNG MAN *standing there*
aghast] What's this?   Friend of yours?

YOUNG MAN. My God!   She was a lady.   That's
all I know about her.

LANGUID LORD. A lady!

>   *The blond and dark gentlemen have slipped from*
>   *the room; and out of the supper-party's distant*
>   *laughter comes suddenly a long, shrill:* "Gone
>   away!"   *And the sound of the horn playing*
>   *the seven last notes of the old song:* "This day a
>   stag must die!"   *From the last note of all the*
>   *sound flies up to an octave higher, sweet and*
>   *thin, like a spirit passing, till it is drowned*
>   *once more in laughter.   The* YOUNG MAN *has*
>   *covered his eyes with his hands;* ARNAUD *is*
>   *crossing himself fervently; the* LANGUID LORD
>   *stands gazing, with one of the dropped gardenias*
>   *twisted in his fingers; and the woman, bending*
>   *over* CLARE, *kisses her forehead.*

CURTAIN.